MW01627220

Praise for Jan Gault's *Play & Grow Rich*

"**Play & Grow Rich** is both inspiring and practical—offering specific steps for those who sincerely want to achieve greater personal & financial riches. I recommend it to all who are interested in becoming more successful doing what they enjoy most!"

Dennis Dalton
General Manager
KLRS Radio

"One of the great masterpieces of all times. I believe it's destined to help millions. Jan Gault has that special ability to guide readers in their entrepreneurial journey with love, encouragement and hope. Even though I have been an entrepreneur for over a decade , **Play & Grow Rich** has opened up new areas of enlightenment to me."

Robert A. Stillman
Publisher and Editor
Lively Arts & Fine Art

"This could be the most valuable book you will ever read to help you discover, establish and fulfill your uniquely creative mission in life."

Dr. Gerald Ewing
Electronics Engineer, Professor
Naval Post Graduate School
Pebble Beach, California

"This is a good book with solid information. On one level you've given the ABCs of doing what you love and attracting riches. There is another level that reaches out and says "This one world is exactly one world and whatsoever I do affects everything else, and the more creatively I do it the more creative this world will be and the more beautiful. I wish to give beauty to the world and I wish to do it not with tongue in cheek but with laughing in my heart".

Joseph S. McVicker
Inventor of Play-Doh

"A brilliant work (or maybe it was play!); light-years beyond *Think & Grow Rich.* Contains the secrets of every successful person I know"

Pat Burns,
PGA Golf Professional
Pebble Beach Golf Links

"Practicing the principles of the book **Play & Grow Rich** gave me a chance to harvest the fruits of success. This book is definitely for the people who desire to enjoy life and grow rich."

Ken Okura,
President
JOY-TAK, Inc.
Pebble Beach, California

"After reading Jan Gault's **Play & Grow Rich** I've been inspired to turn my hobby of golf into a business venture. Instead of just playing golf, now I'm buying golf courses and having an even better time."

Vernon Turnbow
Chairman of the Board
M&T Associates
Scottsdale, Arizona

"...a provocative and worthwhile book, loaded with sound advice on how to achieve personal and financial success."

Dr. Paul M. Pantleo, Ph.D., DDS
Management Consultant
Professional Practice Development
Honolulu, Hawaii

"This is probably the best work I have seen that explains how entrepreneurs think, plan, act, and accomplish their goals. It is absolutely essential for those about to set out on their own, and is both inspiring and practical. Learn from this book, and you will make money, not excuses."

Richard Epley, Ph.D.
Lecturer/Author/Investor

"Now that I've retired from my teaching at University of California, Berkeley, your definitive book is exactly what I need. Excellent ...I keep referring back to it to keep me focused."

Mark Luca, Ph.D.
Who's Who in American Art
President, California Writers Assn.
Marin County, California

"**Play & Grow Rich** will not only help you succeed in business but in life. It should be on everyone's reading list. I liked it very much."

Jerry Luger
Vice President/Investment Associate
Thomas White Co., Inc.
San Francisco

"Dr. Jan Gault's philosophy planted the seeds that helped change my life from an overweight corporate executive caught in the "older employee being put out to pasteur syndrome" to becoming a world-setting athlete after age fifty and an entrepreneur accumulating a Multi-Millionaire net worth status—Thanks Jan."

Jack Riley
President/Owner
Golden Triangle Athletic Club
Walnut Creek, California
Holds the Guinness Book World Record
for most Triathlons in one year.
Author: Designing Quality & Balance in your Life
Host of TV series: Designing Quality Health

"**Play and Grow Rich** is a book for the 90's full of good, useable practical advice loaded with ideas and valuable insights. It's easy to read and forces you to expand your horizons. Put this priceless information into action and it's guaranteed to be an "Insurance Policy Against Being Average".

Edward G. Ciliberti
Real Estate Broker
Carmel, California
President,
Monterey Board of Realtors

"Jan Gault helps you discover the best within yourself and how to turn work into play—and profit!"

William C. Kingman
Broadcast Engineer
KOWL/KRLT RADIO
Lake Tahoe, California

"Thank you for writing **Play & Grow Rich**. I found it very helpful."

Michael Adams
Student

"**Play & Grow Rich** provides an ideal guide for anyone who is dissatisfied with his or her current job or life situation and wants to find a more satisfying way to both make a living and enjoy it. It is particularly good in suggesting ways to organize and manage time and establish priorities to get that extra out of life."

Gini Graham Scott, Ph.D., J.D.
Director
Changemakers and Creative
Communications & Research
Author of over 20 books, including
Resolving Conflict. The Creative Traveler,
Mind Power: Picture Your Way to Success

"This book is about the most important, yet untapped power in the Universe. Jan Gault gives you the tools to make it work for you."

Bob Hamilton
President,
THE NEW RADIO STAR
Carmel, California

"**Free Time** (Dr. Jan Gault's previous book) showed us how to put quality into our leisure time; **Play & Grow Rich** carries this a step further by allowing us to put joy and creativity into our career—**A MUST READ!**"

Alan Stout
Member Pacific Stock Exchange
San Francisco, California

Readers from across the nation respond:

"...explodes the myth that hard work and luck alone will result in success."

Jim R.
Dallas, Texas

"...shows readers how to break loose from Career Tracks that are pounding the life out of them to rediscover their identity and be their own person."

Marilyn T.
Indianapolis, Indiana

"The 271 pages of **Play & Grow Rich** have a special magic about them—like they were written just for me and my situation."

Martin W.
Cleveland, Ohio

"Once in a while, a very important book comes along—Dr. Jan Gault's new release, **Play & Grow Rich**, is one of them."

Patricia S.
Denver, Colorado

PLAY & GROW RICH

HOW TO BREAK FREE FROM THE 9-TO-5 WORLD AND PROFIT FROM WHAT YOU ENJOY MOST

JAN L. GAULT, Ph.D.

PLAY & GROW RICH

Ocean Manor Publishing

First Edition 1989
Second Edition 1992

Library of Congress Cataloging-in-Publication Data

Gault, Jan L.
Play and Grow Rich

1. Success in business. 2. Entrepreneurship.
3. Time management. 4. Leisure. I. Title. II. Title:
Play and grow rich.
HF5386.G26 1989 650.1 88-64117
ISBN 0-923699-00-7

Printed and bound in the United States of America
0 9 8 7 6 5 4 3 2

No profit grows where is no pleasure ta'en

— Shakespeare

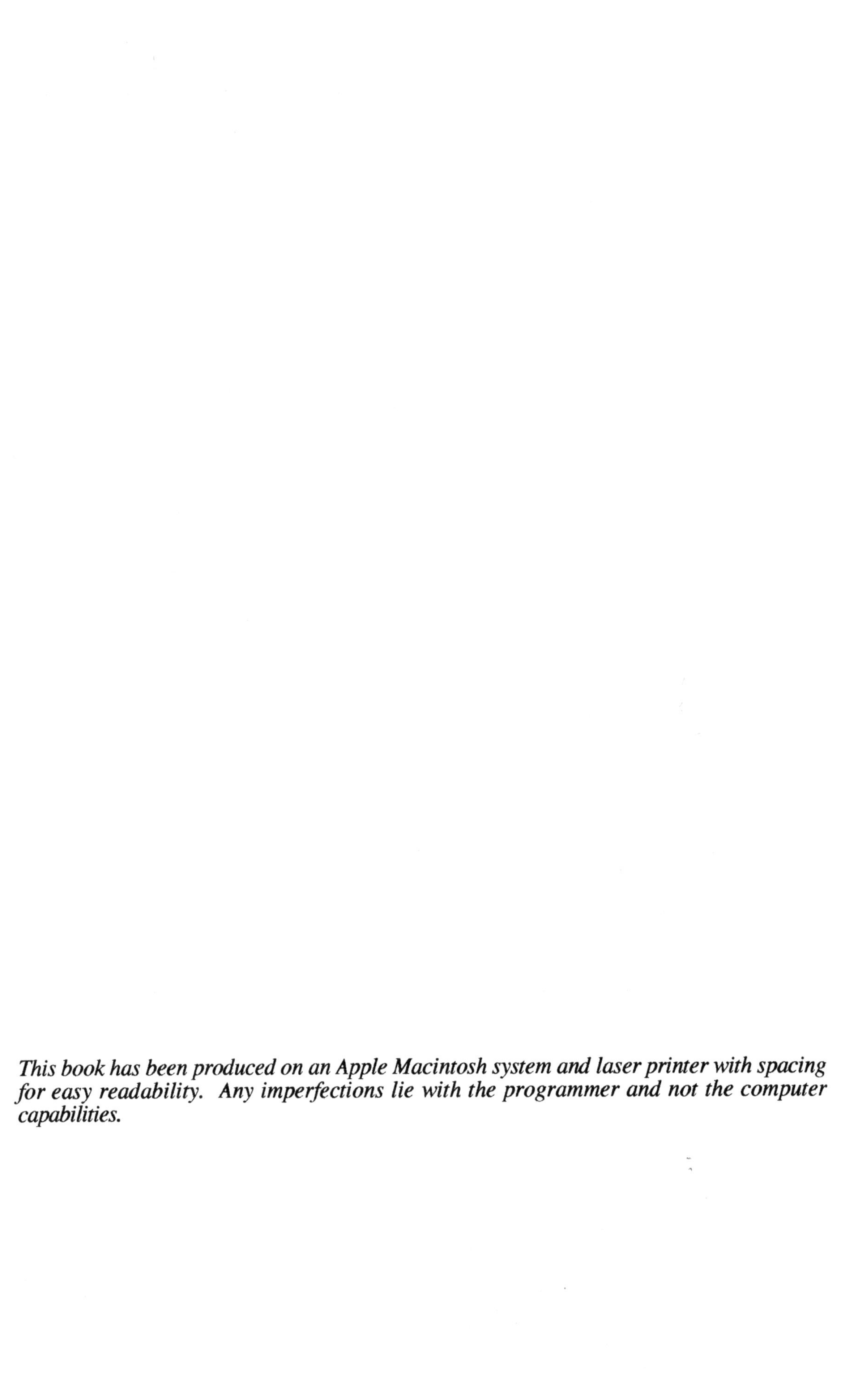

This book has been produced on an Apple Macintosh system and laser printer with spacing for easy readability. Any imperfections lie with the programmer and not the computer capabilities.

Table of Contents

Time Blocks

No. 1: Millionaire Play Sheet
No. 2: Entrepreneur Quiz
No. 3: Entrepreneur Affirmations
No. 4: Investment Procedures
No. 5: Changes in your Consumer Expenditures
No. 6: Temporary Employment Tactics
No. 7: Conflict-Free Living
No. 8: Mind-Bolstering
No. 9: Steps to PPP Discovery & Profit
No. 10: Commitment to Action
No. 11: Ethos Clarification
No. 12: Ethos Polarity Chart
No. 13: Material Prosperity
No. 14: Instilling a Wealth Consciousness
No. 15: "Timelessness"
No. 16: Risk-Taking
No. 17: "Millionaire Play Sheet" Update
No. 18: Setting Up External Props
No. 19: Endless Tape Dynamics
No. 20: Voices of Authority
No. 21: Triumph Over Down Days

Illustrations

This book is dedicated to you, the reader,
with love and encouragement toward your
adventure in entrepreneurship

Acknowledgments

I would like to acknowledge the handful of rare and wonderful problem-free tenants who occupied my properties during the production of this book, allowing me the time to devote to research and writing. Especially, I'd like to thank Mike Dunne.with U.S. Air Lines at my Lover's Point, Pacific Grove property for never calling me with a single problem and making rent payments long before they were due; Robert Czomba at Pacific Grove for putting in his time and money to make the many improvements to my property; Bob Remington in my Marina four-plex for his positive attitude and helpfulness; Tom Peter of my Monterey apartment unit for his understanding and good humor when water from a broken pipe flooded the place; Ed Teliczan who occupied my Carmel property for doing his best to pay the rent even when it was not easy; Craig and Connie Luigart at 17th St. for treating my property like their own; and last, Steve and Jani Doak at my Pebble Beach property for their beautiful upkeep and enthusiastic willingness to show the home to prospective buyers that went far beyond what was required.

In addition, I want to thank all those entrepreneurs interviewed for this book, in particular, Richard Clements, architect and builder at Big Sur for the gracious interview and reflections on his success as an entrepreneur; Bob Casperian of Marin County, a sailboat enthusiast who is living life to the fullest; Alan Stout, options trader, for introducing me to the many excellent books and tapes; Joseph McVicker, Inventor of Play-Doh for his careful reading and insightful comments for the 2nd edition; and others who shared their experiences and information.

A special acknowledgment to William J. Finch for his research assistance and to Karen Davis for her editing suggestions. Also Marvin Kooken of Computer Base for his courtesy and helpfulness.

Finally, a tribute to those friends and family members for their moral support and encouragement: Frank R., Alan S., Ernie M., Dennis R., Stanton F., M. Allen L.; Charles Gault, Laura Gault, Ken Gault, Tracy Gault, Seth. Ian, Ryan, Stephanie, Micah, Christina, and mother, Mary Belle Vance.

Responsibility for any errors or other shortcomings in the book is mine alone.

Introduction

Many writers today speak of the decline of the work ethic and attempt to link it to America's drop in productivity as well as a dozen other ills facing our nation. On both counts this view is misleading. For a large part of the population the work ethic is still very much in effect. Secondly, a fundamental premise on which it rests—long hours, hard work and frugal living will result in the riches of life—does not hold up under inspection.

The work ethic in Western Culture can be traced back as far as the Medieval Period. Following the fall of the Roman Empire, a reaction to the hedonism and pleasure-seeking of the Romans set in. Any leisure time was viewed with derision. Hard work became valued for its own sake. In fact, for the majority of people, there was little choice: long hours and hard labor were a necessary way of life. The small amount of free time available was spent in rest and restoration for another day's work.

Leisure or personal free time was never thought of in its own right, but was merely seen as something incidental and of little significance. Life centered around work and survival needs. In the 17th Century as Calvinism grew in popularity, this attitude toward work and leisure became even more entrenched. Calvin's teachings not only implied that honesty and hard work would help one to move out of poverty and misery, but that one's very salvation was at stake. Perhaps if you truly worked hard enough and long enough you would be saved from damnation. There was always the element of uncertainty, impending doom, and the associated guilt-anxiety foreboding; if you took time to enjoy yourself, somehow you might miss out.

Economic conditions have changed dramatically since our early history, moving us through an agricultural community to an industrial nation, up to our present high-tech information society. Nevertheless, the "psychological lag" has not kept pace and caught up to our new era of leisure. We feel guilty if we are not continually busy doing something. Attempting to sit down and relax after work elicits traces of guilt and anxiety because there is always something we could be doing. "Ought to's" and "should do's" dominate our life, giving us little peace of mind. This of course is a trap because life is always half undone—there will forever be things that are incomplete and need doing. We have not come to terms with the work ethic.

The simple truth is: the work ethic is no longer valid in our society (if ever it was). Hard work and honesty alone are unlikely to result in either financial independence or the life-satisfaction, understanding, and spiritual fulfillment we so desperately desire.

All you need do is look around you to see this confirmed. How many people have worked hard and honestly all their lives only to wind up at a subsistence level in later retirement years? Few of our senior citizens have funds to adequately provide for their basic needs. And hundreds of thousands who have sought security in a job find themselves laid off after fifteen or more years of service. The vast majority of people consider themselves doing well if they manage to put their children through college and have a few dollars left for a vacation once a year.

It is usually not until midlife and our observation that we have achieved neither the successes hoped for nor the elusive sense of self-worth and meaning we crave that the Puritan work ethic is called into question. Many factors are responsible for personal and financial success, irrespective of job earnings, work dedication and long hours. Both your consumer habits and investment programs (or lack of) play a role in the accumulation of wealth and personal well-being. Astuteness in the marketplace, knowing how to raise capital, using sound money-managing strategies and tax shelters all have a bearing on your prosperity and peace of mind.

The key factor, however, relating to your prosperity and well-being is the sense of purpose, direction and spirit of freedom you bring to life. Those who achieve great success, whether financial or personal success, do so because they *love* what they're doing. They pursue the kind of goals that are right for them, that align with their personality, interests and deepest values. Then they are able to go all out, make a full commitment, take the risk and progress swiftly without a lot of doubts about whether they're taking the best course.

You will never be highly successful at something you cannot get excited and enthused about. Without a dream and a vision, all the clutter and distractions about you will create too many detours. Life will not hang together right to keep you focused, on target and progressing consistently toward your goals.

If a goal is drudgery, you'll continually have a fight on your hands to do it; it will be a constant struggle, an on-going battle with yourself. Look at any highly successful artist, musician, writer, inventor, singer or scientist and you will find this element of play: a total absorption, passion, perhaps even obsession with their "love".

This does not mean that some aspects of what you do will not be demanding or tough at times. What it means is that *in spite of* whatever comes up and gets in the way of your goal, you will continue to have the zest, the energy and natural enthusiasm to carry you through and keep you going...the emotional, playful 'pack' on your back that lightens your load rather than weighting you down.

Did you ever watch a child stacking blocks? The blocks have his or her total attention and interest. S/he is totally absorbed in the challenge of creating a new height with each block. Then suddenly without warning they all come tumbling down. At first stunned, the child sees the humor in the situation, claps his hands, laughs and starts building again, this time correcting for mistakes and creating an even higher pyramid. When Thomas Edison's laboratory equipped with innovations representing thousands of hours of love-labor burned down, he was asked, "Whatever will you do?" His reply was swift and firm, "We will start building again in the morning". With a clear vision, a dream, enthusiasm and total commitment, nothing is likely to prevent you from achieving whatever it is you want from life.

Preface

Time structuring for wealth

We have grown up believing that all we need to make a killing is a good idea and the money to see it through. The most crucial variable, however, is neither the idea nor the money, but your own state of mind together with the time methods you put into practice. Before quitting work and giving yourself twenty-four hours a day to call your own, you need to establish a solid habit pattern of "time structuring".

Throughout life, the majority of us have walked into ready-made educational and work structures. We have had little experience approaching time from an individual standpoint with respect to our own values and personal objectives. In modern society, for the most part, both the time boundaries and the content of our hours have been laid out for us. At school and in the workplace we have been told when to come and when to go. Although more flexible school and work schedules have been introduced in recent years, generally speaking, we start our days at prescribed times and end them at designated hours. How we fill these hours is largely governed by what is required to merit good grades in school, get a decent salary on the job and be in line for the next promotion. While we are offered many choices such as the selection of our major field of study and where we are to be employed, the important parameters have already been set: the underlying values, goals and objectives of the educational institutions and firms we join have been pre-established with the individual time slots waiting to be filled accordingly.

Given this history of having the bulk of your time structured by others for so many years, stepping out on your own without preparation is rarely advisable, and can be hazardous to your mental, physical and financial health. It can be compared with throwing a baby in the water and hoping he'll swim. If not, someone is standing by to pull him out. As an entrepreneur, no one is likely to be standing by to bail you out. Until you gain the know-how, strength and momentum that comes from purposeful structuring of your personal time, the minutes, hours and days can all too easily slip away unproductively. And as they do, you will find that your ambition, enthusiasm and motivation are slipping away also, leaving you feeling at odds with both yourself and society.

Taking full charge of your own time to successfully channel your actions toward specific entrepreneurial projects and still keep your balance in all the other vital dimensions of your life requires fine mind-tuning and correct practice. Most of us flub up in our attempts to structure even two hours of discretionary time a day toward our goals, much less twenty-four. We are all too prone to the distractions that come up and temptations that pull us off course. Procrastination and idle activities keep us from our purpose. Before you leave your job structure and work routine behind, therefore, you want to become adept at building time habits in line with your enterprise objectives.

In each chapter of this book you are going to learn to build time blocks. You will start off gradually, taking one-half hour periods initially. These are increased as we go along until you are comfortable with three hours per day and five hours on Saturday or Sunday. Once you have mastered the art of structuring twenty hours per week of free time toward your entrepreneurial pursuits, you are ready to quit work and put in full time for yourself.

At each stage, a more advanced time-empowering step will be provided for your prosperity and riches. As you begin to build time blocks, you build dollars.

Your entrepreneurial time blocks are made up of three critical aspects:

(1)Reinforcement of a playful, purposeful spirit.

(2)Creative behavior and reaching definite decision points.

(3)Action resulting in entrepreneurial innovations and profit.

The first and foremost time building blocks are the development of a playful, purposeful spirit. Without it, everything else falls apart. This is the wind beneath your wings that keeps you soaring no matter what. It is the energy, enthusiasm, thrust and driving power behind every action, and over, around and through each obstacle. It is the staying power when everything goes wrong. Cultivating your innermost playful, creative spirit gives joy and meaning to every endeavor regardless of how minor or seemingly insignificant it appears on the surface. When the details of running a business threaten to wear you down, this underlying energy will see you through.

1
The Occupational Malaise

"The deepest personal defeat suffered by human beings is constituted by the difference between what one was capable of becoming and what one has in fact become."

—Ashley Montagu

1
Career Pipedreams

"Most people spend most of their days doing what they do not want to do in order to earn the right, at times, to do what they may desire."
—JOHN MASON BROWN

Ideally, you should be receiving income from what you enjoy most. Yet studies increasingly confirm that the majority of people are dissatisfied with their work or work conditions. This dissatisfaction is not limited to on-line assembly employees, but includes persons from across a large segment of occupational groups and professions: corporate executives, bankers, physicians, attorneys, accountants, teachers, secretaries, computer analysts, programmers and others.

We roll over in bed in the morning and wish we could just stay there. And how we love to get away from our place of employment! You have only to look at the happy, smiling faces all about you on a Friday afternoon before a three-day weekend.

There are many reasons for our discontent with the current state of affairs. A look at some of the contributing factors will help you crystalize where you stand and the best course of action to take.

Unrealistic expectations

A major source of frustration is the excessive career expectations held in our society. We expect work to meet our complex multitude of needs. We look for a job that will offer challenge, let us use our creative abilities, be fulfilling, give us the recognition we crave, plus be interesting and enjoyable. At the same time, we expect our employer to take care of our needs for financial security, provide health and life insurance benefits, a good pension plan, a liberal expense allowance and lots of perks.

And when our job does not measure up, as few jobs can, we become disenchanted and start dreaming about the time when we will have a better job, maybe even going back to school to train for another kind of career. The solution to our problems, we believe, is in finding the right occupation.

The search for self-fulfillment

For decades we have looked to our careers and the work setting in our quest for meaning and self-fulfillment. Writers continue to lament the rise of technology, impersonality of the computer age and loss of meaning within the work environment. However, even in the best of jobs, whether in years past or present, our search for self-expression and creative outlets comes up short. It is an unrealistic stance.

I hear this often among the men and women in my consulting practice. Physicians, attorneys, high-tech managers, teachers and other professionals confess that a major part of their duties are perfunctory, routine and just plain boring. The biggest chunk of the day is frequently spent in semi-productive meetings, wading through stacks of paperwork, and dealing with people not of one's choosing. If we add to these the thousands of other jobs in existence with even less opportunities for need-fulfillment, it is difficult to see why we continue to cling to our career pipedreams.

Personal goals vs. employer goals

Another source of dissatisfaction, although it is not easily articulated, is the match between your personal goals and your firm's interests. The bottom line from most employers' point of view is whether widget profits are up to snuff. In assisting them toward this goal via your assigned duties you hope also to have some of your personal desires met.

For example, let's say you feel a strong need for challenge in your life. It was one of the things you listed on your job application when you sought your present position. Recently your supervisor gave you a tough project to put together in a short two-week period. This represents at least one kind of challenge.

The question to ask is, "What proportion of the total time directed toward my employer's goals is consistent with my own goals?" And secondly, "Are those high priority personal needs which are not being adequately provided for on the job nurtured during nonwork time allocation?" (See Figure 1)

If you are working eight hours or more per day at your place of employment as well as using a substantial amount of nonwork hours for employer-related activities (commuting, shopping for work attire, reading materials, attending business luncheons and going to required seminars and conferences), there is probably little time left over for personal goals. Unless an appreciable match exists between your objectives and your firm's, you want to seriously consider how much time you are spending on your employer's goals at the expense of your own.

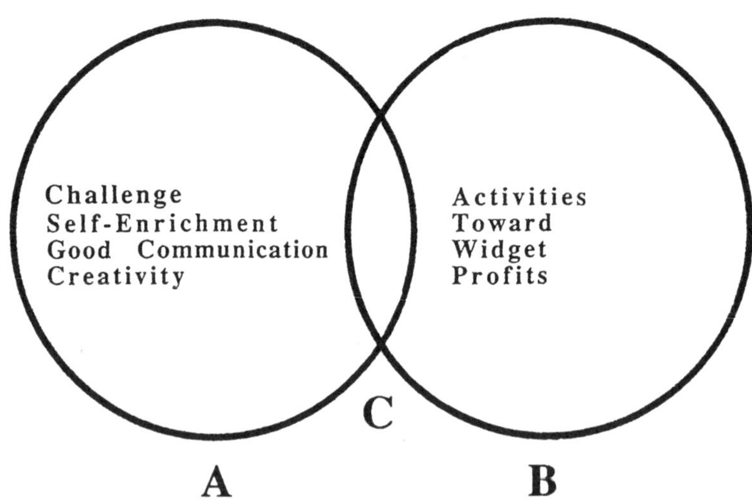

A = Personal Goals
B = Employer Goals
C = Overlap

Figure 1: Match Between Personal Goals & Employer Goals

Ask yourself if the bulk of your waking time is oriented solely toward your employer's aim and whether the monetary compensation and perks received offset the price you are paying by denying any personal goals.

Not coming to terms with this lack of individual need fulfillment is likely to result in an on-going latent malcontent that surfaces periodically and especially during times of stress.

The ethical issue

A related issue is how closely your firm's involvements and practices align or clash with your own value system. This carries with it all the questions that were raised so dramatically back in the sixties. Although these appear to have been shelved or at least temporarily quietened, the basic problem remains to be settled.

Misgivings and uneasiness here may center around a conflict about your firm concerning the particular product produced, service rendered, production methods, marketing procedures or applications. Depending on your attitudes and value judgments, any number of items could be objectionable, from processed foods, meat, alcoholic beverages, coffee, cigarettes, to certain pharmaceutical products and military weapons. Some simplistic examples of potentially tension-evoking work settings would be a vegetarian employed by a butcher, a nonsmoker promoting cigarettes and a teetotaler waiting on tables in a cocktail lounge. With giant conglomerate industries, mergers and information control found in business today, few positions and choices are so clearcut. Most employees do not even know what all their firms are involved in.

Indirect services and interests that support or perpetuate what are seen as objectionable products and procedures further cloud the picture. A management consulting firm whose major clients are from the tobacco, oil or utility industry would be one example. Questionable sources for funding of a firm's activities add to the confusion.

The problem is not confined to big business but permeates the professions and their supporting staff as well. Attorneys and accountants in the private sector have told me they often feel that they're working on the wrong side of the fence. Falling back on cliches such as, "It's all part of the job", "If I didn't do it, someone else would", and "That's the way the system works" do little to assuage guilt. One prominent San Francisco attorney who has been practicing law for seventeen years told me, "In all honesty, I don't see how anyone could be in this profession for more than five years and say they liked it, or felt good about what goes on."

Physicians also frequently find themselves in a compromising situation by relying mainly on the pharmaceutical industry's recommendations for prescribing drugs to patients. Unable to keep up with or adequately evaluate all the new products on the market, they fall back on drug sales personnel who cater to them, and information from articles appearing in medical journals largely supported by advertisements from the drug industry. Although many physicians confess to having misgivings about their selection process here, and not properly evaluating the side-effects of drugs prescribed for patients, they feel boxed in by time constraints and demands made upon them.

As a nation, we are known for our ability to live and work in a world of startling inconsistencies and contradictions. This is not to say, however, that we do not suffer because of it. Nearly every person I've spoken with from a diverse assortment of occupations expressed concern about the current situation but were mostly at a loss as to what could be done. Attempting to adhere to your personal standards in making an occupational choice for a large and growing body of industry and professional groups is nigh impossible. Even thorough research of prospective employers would no doubt prove futile. By the time you finished checking them out, the firm's circumstances may have been changed by a merger or other events.

One Lockheed physicist with pacifist convictions told me that he was able to keep peace with himself by refusing to work on any projects that were directly related to warfare. At best, our choices represent only partial solutions insofar as we are bound to the occupational hierarchy. For the majority of the employed population we are more likely to see a careful neglect over confronting any value issues whenever our source of livelihood is at stake. Or, when the problem does present itself, we find ourselves rationalizing it away as best we can.

Unfortunately, rationalizations out of ignorance, economic necessity, or an ill-defined personal value system, fail to bail us out of this dilemma. Attempting to sell yourself on putting in eight hours a day, year after year, for the greater part of your life, to produce and promote products and services which are in opposition to those things you believe in shakes at the very foundation of existence.

Misplaced corporate loyalty

One of the most effective means of control is when a person, group or entity is able to command your undivided loyalty. This is a more powerful motivator of employee behavior than salary increases, fringe benefits or even work safety factors. The forms that loyalty takes and how it evolves is a whole topic in itself, in essence, however, it is putting the best interests of another over those of your own. With reference to the work setting, loyalty generally comes about to the degree that you identify with your position and firm. "I am a Pacific Telephone computer analyst." "I am an IBM man." "I am a Bank of America teller."

Loyalty to our employer is often an extension of habit patterns developed early in the educational process. As children, we would go all out doing the work required to please our teachers and get the pat on the back or 'A' for performance. By high school or college, you probably reached a point where you became more discriminating and weighed your options in terms of time spent and desired outcomes. For instance, you may have decided to spend less time on your economics and political science courses, earn Cs or Bs instead of As, and use the time left over to give priority to something else: another course you valued more, a personal relationship or new social experience.

Situations in the work setting can be tougher. If you have just taken a new position with XYZ company in Silicon Valley where everyone is working twelve hours a day including Saturdays, you may find it difficult not to conform regardless of the value of other commitments in your life. Even more complicated are circumstances where you have been with a firm for several years and are part of a work force that is putting in long hours. Though you are now beginning to question whether this is what you want, breaking the pattern without penalty is next to impossible. This is especially true among a growing number of high-tech firms where there is little sense of reverse loyalty from employer to employee. If you cannot do the job, put in the hours and handle the stress, there is always someone else around to take your place. You are an expendable cog and know it. Besides, you have high mortgage payments to make, car payments, insurance premiums, and are trying to sock away enough dollars to cover the rising college costs for your kids.

Running the risk of getting fired is out of the question. And this is where the frustration comes in.

The predicament so many of us find ourselves in is jumping ambitiously into a "promising career opportunity" with blinders in respect to the impact on other dimensions of our life, not to mention what we are capable of accomplishing if we put in even a fraction of those hours on our own behalf.

Failure to reach a conscious decision point and come to terms with any necessary personal goal sacrifices before you are caught up in such a situation can only result in tension, bad health and bad temper. The turnover rate and burnout rate in Silicon Valley, for example, among employees and the impact on spouses and children has been well-documented. A similar trend is predicted in other parts of the nation. Most of the high-tech people I have spoken with have a somewhat vague plan of getting in, building up capital, and getting out within a short period of time. Data suggests that no such thing happens. Consumer purchases, debts and obligations rise along with income.

Be aware that long hours of work per se are not the villain to mental or physical health. When you are involved in work which you genuinely enjoy, and where there are no nagging personal conflicts, you can continue almost indefinitely without fatigue or any ill effects. What's damaging is the frustration that results from having unresolved conflicts about your commitments and loyalties. Turning over the greater part of your time to an employer's interests to produce a new or better widget, even a good and valuable widget, cannot be justified if it negates another higher priority goal (your spouse leaves you; your kids are growing up and you hardly know them; your body is falling apart). Only when you have a sound perspective about your values, personal goals and how your work fits into the overall plan of your living will you be able to unravel these confusions.

The other problem encountered in corporate loyalty and having your identity tied so tightly to the firm you are employed by is the personal insecurity. If the whole thrust of your existence is wrapped up in the position you hold and your performance in that position then when you are not performing or your job is no more, you are no more (or at the very least have diminished value). This happens when a particular job is phased out by an employer, when you are fired or laid off, when you quit and are in-between jobs, and when you retire. Even a promotion, where you are bumped up to a new position, is threatening until you again "establish yourself".

The malignant trend of the occupational network

Another factor that has played host to our occupational uneasiness is an increasing awareness of many of the problems inherent in the structure and functioning of our major associations and corporations. Whether it's the medical profession largely subsidized by the pharmaceutical industry, the chemical and utility industries with their threat to personal and national safety, or the polluting effects of the automobile and oil industries, their negative impact on individual, social and ecological health has become all too evident.

We can no longer shrug off giving eight (or even six) hours a day over the course of a lifetime to entities who are not necessarily "bad guys" but whose affairs have simply gotten out of hand in certain respects. As more and more people are recognizing the ways in which these corporate bodies are directly and indirectly increasing the likelihood of nuclear war, ecological destruction, human disease and suffering, we have begun questioning how we might restructure our personal-work lifestyles so that we no longer support the sustenance and expansion of these structures. At the same time we must take care not to be thrown into a marginal poverty existence where we are forever scrambling to put food on the table and have no time, energy or resources left to create constructive alternatives.

Today, with the increase in leisure time and freedom from dawn-to-dusk survival-work-patterns, we are in a position to better reflect on our role, responsibility and the kind of individual response to make in view of this apparent impasse. As we observe the momentum of vested interests (millions, even billions of dollars at stake) and the difficulties in disentangling these giant entities in a way that will not throw the world into utter chaos, we are correctly looking to ourselves and entrepreneurial options in an attempt to intelligently and creatively improve the situation.

You may protest what such a seemingly remote and grandiose goal has to do with your individual prosperity. This will become clearer in subsequent chapters. As you shall see, each mind step you take in advancing your world perspective of the role you play in the total scheme of things is intimately related to your personal prosperity.

The impact of occupation on your lifestyle

The career you choose, position you hold and particular firm you are employed by permeates your whole life style. It typically dictates where you live and commute and how you dress and eat. It can influence the social organizations you belong to, what you read and who you spend your time with. Even your sense of identity and how you think and feel about yourself is frequently tied to your occupation and position.

A divorced, middle-aged marketing executive with a large insurance firm in Los Angeles provides a striking example. Year in and year out Bruce has learned to wear the "uniform": Subtle herringbone and pin-striped grey or wheat colored suits; solid or thin-striped light blue and white shirts; high black or blue socks with only plain toe or wingtip black and brown shoes. While the expert image consultants may differ in their opinions, it is an accepted fact within the corporate world that clothes make a difference in obtaining promotions, securing contracts and personal status. Bruce admits to making referrals and giving business to those associates who play by the rules and dress in the proper attire. "After all", he tells me, "baseball players wouldn't go onto the field out of uniform".

In his nonwork hours Bruce is on the board of Rotary Club and attends various social functions connected with his business in order to maintain the right contacts. He describes these as "boring obligations". Over the last five years Bruce has had affairs with two secretaries and three sales representatives he happened to meet in the course of his work activities. None have proven satisfying, but someday he hopes to get lucky and happen into a good relationship.

Like many of the employed people I have counseled, Bruce lives for the weekends. He has bought a house convenient to the office where he works to avoid a long commute, although he complains that "the neighborhood sucks", and he stays away as much as possible. By the weekend Bruce is ready to head for the mountains in his Cessna 182 private airplane, shucking his uniform as well as his sobriety. Drinking is the order of the day, starting with three Bloody Marys on Saturday morning and continuing with a steady input of Beck's beer until Monday morning when it's time to sober up, fly back to urban living and get back into the "grueling" work routine.

Lack of control over your own time

A primary source of worker dissatisfaction is lack of control over your own time. This occurs not only within all those 9-to-5 hours, but is contained in the mind remnants of the day that come home with you: problems left unresolved, colleague confrontations, the undone "to do" lists, and thoughts of tomorrow's demands. These left-over internal work rumblings may invade your consciousness to the extent that even your nonwork hours turn out to be never truly free.

In an effort to quell, bury or dump these mind remnants, we may seek refuge and relief in beer, cathartic outbursts with a mate, or other temporary resorts. Under these conditions it is no wonder we have difficulty developing and implementing our entrepreneurial ideas!

Although most occupations offer some leeway and choice about how you spend your time on the job, overall, employees are bound to fulfilling the tasks associated with the goals of their firm. If in addition there is little match between performance of your employer's goals and on-the-job progression toward your personal objectives, malcontent is twofold. This coupled with a situation where you are putting in time for a firm whose products, services or activities are objectionable to your code of ethics makes matters unpleasant indeed.

One of the most critical factors for mental and physical well-being is having control over your own time. This means having the power to make those decisions vital to your best interests in all areas of your life.

Cutting the Occupational Umbilical Cord

We have talked about fundamental sources of career dissatisfaction making little mention of the long list of daily complaints heard regularly among the working population. Your frustration may also stem from a variety of these more specific on-the-job conditions: petty office politics; game-playing tactics by co-workers, subordinates and superiors; personality clashes and squabbles; being passed over for a deserved promotion; doing outstanding work on a project without receiving any recognition; putting together a program that saved your firm thousands of dollars for which your boss claimed credit; having impossible deadlines to meet; not being enough a part of the decision and policy-making process; social slights by office personnel; a polluted work environment; and an unsafe work setting.

A number of the positive thought advocates would have us believe that all we need do to resolve our work dissatisfactions is to focus on the bright side. "After all", it is argued, "you are getting paid for your time and receiving a measure of security and compensation. Why not just look at the rewards and benefits?

As the previous pronouncements suggest, the problem is not quite so simple or clearcut. There is a need for a major personal-time and employer-time value shift, lifestyle reorientation and overhauling of some of our habit patterns which have put occupation in the limelight. (See Figures 2 and 3)

EXTINCT MODEL

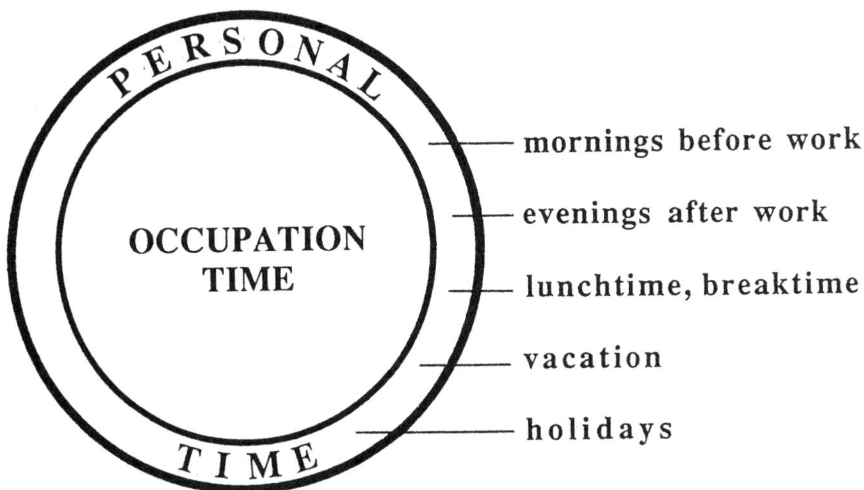

Figure 2: Personal Time as Incidental to Occupation

MODEL UPDATE

Figure 3: Occupation as Incidental to Personal Time

The goal is to reconstruct your time space from the starting point of personal autonomy so that the spin-offs of your choices (financial gain, relationships, health-fitness and self-enrichment) flow naturally from an individual value nucleus. Instead of constantly finding yourself in a situation where you must adapt and compromise within the confines of today's occupational framework, as the new entrepreneur you have the opportunity to take full charge of your time and create a better world for yourself and others.

Although I have been a bit hard on the drawbacks of traditional work, it is absolutely imperative that you let go of any lingering doubts about somehow "missing out" on some unknown ideal career. Until this becomes firmly established in your mind, the lure of the phantom glamour career will continue to loom before you as you read the want ads promising "challenge, opportunity and rapid advancement". This dissipates your energy and keeps you from giving your full attention to new business ventures.

The occupational malaise is the most menacing time-devourer standing between you and success. You want to get rid of this impeding dragon once and for all so that you are free to romp in the playground of your dreams and endeavors.

To lay a solid foundation for success on your own, settle with yourself now the extent of the occupational hazard so there is no turning back. Making a full commitment as an entrepreneur means doing away with any qualifier-type thinking such as, "If things don't work out...", and "just in case, I can always go back to...". It is necessary to burn your occupational bridges, give up the myth of the ideal phantom career waiting in the wings and go all out in achieving riches under your own auspices.

We have been talking about all the things you don't want, but what about the positive side, those things you do want? Before picking up this book, you might already have had some inkling of what you would like to do on your own. Though you probably hadn't laid out all the reasons why, deep in your gut you have felt that all is not well on the workfront and would like to get off the merry-go-round. The problem is that you are exhausted at the end of the day and are able to give only half a mind to how you are going to make the transition, ease out of your present job and into something else. You have come up with a few ideas, perhaps have even drawn up tentative plans and are waiting for conditions to be right.

Before you take the plunge, you would like to have feedback on your ideas and where the best opportunities are found. You want to know what the chances of success are, the financial risk, and how to get started. A dozen questions come to mind. "Where can I raise capital?" "Should I quit my job right away?" "How will I survive until my business starts paying off?" "What kinds of problems should I be prepared for?" "Do I need any particular training or skills?"

The question that comes up most, however, in one form or another is: "Do I really have what it takes to be successful?" This is a reasonable question and deserves an answer. With the high percentage of new businesses failing annually, what assurance do you have that yours is going to be one that makes it? What is that special something which tilts the scale toward success over failure? Does it have to do with nothing more than the whims of the marketplace or is the deciding factor found in some magic blend of personality characteristics?

New business downfalls have been attributed to everything from insufficient start-up capital, poor management and bad timing to placing the blame on tight competition, government regulation and the political situation. You may well ask, "Am I going to be able to handle all the problems that arise? Certainly I want to 'try it on my own' but in leaving my present job am I going to be trading in one set of headaches for an even bigger batch of problems?"

The answers to these questions lie in the route you take and your own unique approach. For this we turn to Chapter Two, "The Entrepreneurial Challenge".

2
The Entrepreneurial Challenge

"(A person's) main task in life is to give birth to him (or her) self."

—ERICH FROMM

How many instances have we seen where someone we know has worked for years, grumbling and discontent about their employment only to quit, retire or lose their job, and instead of feeling relief and delight, throw themselves into a panic and despair. "Whatever will I do?" they wail. Rather than facing their newfound freedom with an anticipation of new opportunities and confidence in their ability to create better circumstances for themselves, they are tortured with doubts, fears and self-reprisals.

Most of us do not have the foggiest notion about what steps to begin taking up the path to successful entrepreneurship. We believe all we need is a good idea, a break, someone to back us financially and we're on our way. Until that lucky day we trudge along with the majority of the population in the obsolete employment circle, our whole energy thrust spent in making the rounds to "find a job". Even as we become settled into a new job our eyes are peeled toward finding something better, perhaps with a fatter salary, greater benefits and more security. Rarely does it occur to us that we have the power to create our own job, whether in or out of the workplace, and live according to our own mandates.

To assist you in making the transition from employee to entrepreneur, in this chapter we look at some of the changes which are about to take place under your new life's course. At the end of the chapter you will be given a short quiz to assess your present bent for entrepreneurial success. As you begin thinking, feeling and acting like an entrepreneur, all the occupational hazards that have infringed on your freedom and financial independence are going to rapidly dissipate. In their place you will find the replenishment of those vital personality needs within you crying out for attention. Let's recapitulate some of these.

Appropriate challenges and creative outlets

Your expectations for finding challenge and opportunities for creative expression on the job were largely thwarted because you neither had complete control over the content of your work nor how your time was put together. Now, as you head out on your own, *you* are the party in charge, selecting your own work projects and structuring each day as you decide. Challenge, creative outlets and future profits are all in your hands. Most promising of all, these happy expectations can be met by following the methods and procedures laid out in the pages to come.

Well-placed loyalty

As an entrepreneur, your loyalty need no longer be misplaced. Your faith is right where it should be: in yourself, your own talents, special skills and abilities. You needn't be beholden to anyone simply because they have the power to fire you, promote you or act to make your days miserable. In business for yourself you are going to have many "bosses", i.e., persons you need to deal with as you go about your affairs, but the difference is in your latitude of choice. For the most part, you will be calling the shots and can place your confidence and trust in people of your own selection.

A solid ethical stance

One of the most satisfying aspects of being on your own is the control you have over any value questions and issues that arise. When there is a grey area and a tough decision needs to be made, you are exempt from the threat of harsh reprisals hanging over your head if you take a position out of step with your employer's requirements. On your own, you might lose a contract on occasion by sticking to what you believe in, but generally you can count on coming out ahead. Best of all, *you* are in the pilot's seat and can stay true to those values you cherish without compromising yourself and others.

And there is no better feeling than knowing that you are a part of the stream of positive changes betiding the world today and the impact of many individuals such as yourself is producing a powerful ripple effect for future generations.

Personal goal fulfillment

On your own, with control over your daily activities, you are free of the conflict between your personal goals and employer's goals as experienced in the occupational setting. Now the match is perfect: you are at liberty to set up and allocate your time exactly as is consistent with your priorities. For example, at one period in your life the emphasis may be on establishing better personal relationships. At another stage you might want to go all out to improve your health and maintain a demanding physical fitness program. During still another phase of your life, spiritual development may take precedence.

At this reading, it is probable that you are putting financial independence at the top of the list. As the importance of one goal in your life changes, you have the power to adjust your time blocks accordingly. There is no longer the tug and pull and frustration of trying to fit your personal success goals and objectives into a time frame of someone else's choosing.

During the onset of entrepreneurship, however, it is mandatory that you know where you stand in relation to each of your life goals in order to minimize potential conflicts. You do not want to be at arms with yourself. This topic will be taken up in more detail later, giving you specific methods for achieving clarity here. For now, recognize that the spotlight is on learning the fine art of entrepreneurship and structuring your time as such. It is from this nucleus that everything else is to be viewed and put into proper perspective.

Control over your own time

The major difference that comes with a shift in focus from working at a job to entrepreneurship is that you have the freedom to take complete charge of your time. You can put the minutes and hours together in any way you choose, as is best suited to your personality. You can work six months, complete a project, then reward yourself with three months off. If you are not a morning person, you can work afternoons and evenings. You can elect to work weekends and take a day off during the week to shop, run errands, go to the beach, ski or play tennis when there is less congestion and crowds.

No more must you stretch and stress your system to fit into jobs that are only available during fixed time slots. Now at last you can march to the beat of your own rhythms to become involved in those endeavors and projects that align with your particular interests and personal philosophy.

Instigating Change

The difficult part is changing your former habit patterns and putting together your time in such a way that propels you directly toward worthwhile, profitable goals. Mostly, we move through life circumventing our primary and most important missions. Every now and then we get close to where we would like to be, feel great, and then drift right back off course again. Always, we have some sense of where we are going and what we are doing, but the bulk of our time is diffused and wasted, leaving us feeling drained and off track.

Just how do you get started, stay on course, and create those habit patterns that support and build up your momentum? Today there are over 170 universities offering courses in entrepreneurship. Almost anyone can learn the details and techniques of starting and running a business. Studying and putting into practice how to formulate a business plan, franchise, incorporate, obtain funding and keep your books in order are relatively easy. And anyone can read the many entrepreneurial books on the market and learn hundreds of ideas that have made and will continue to make money. It's easy to accumulate the factual data necessary to set up your business enterprise.

Why then don't we see more successful entrepreneurs? Fewer than twelve per cent of those persons who go into business for themselves make it. And less than one per cent make it big. The failure rate is staggering. With all the information at hand, what goes wrong? Is it simply a matter of blind luck and fate? Or is there an extra something which distinguishes top entrepreneurs from those who are forever limping along? If so, what is this magic ingredient and how do you get it?

The happy news is, "No, it is definitely not a matter of chance, fate or how the cards fall." Whether you become a successful entrepreneur and achieve riches is not written in the stars but is almost *entirely up to you.* If this is truly what you desire, the opportunity is there for the taking. Fortunately, those mysterious elements that separate the successful from the unsuccessful can be learned just as concrete factual data is learned. It is simply a bit trickier.

Throughout the pages of this book you'll see a way of living and being emerging; though hazy at first and even confusing sometimes, as you begin to capture its essence and break with old patterns, you will find yourself being swept up in an exciting momentum. The pinnacle of entrepreneurship is being able to literally call your time your own and move about naturally, freely and joyfully within the space you have created. Having a life of time turned over to you, however, can be damnation or glory. Like a child being handed a dozen new toys all at once, leaving work to suddenly inherit unlimited hours that can be filled up in hundreds of different ways is overwhelming if you are unprepared.

Preparation for this giant feat entails changes in your thought stream, emotional state and spiritual world as well as the many external phenomena impacting on your life. You will discover how to take over your time space in a way that your whole being meshes in unison with the forces of the universe to let you leap to new levels of awareness and wealth. This is no small matter, and is the most ambitious task you shall ever encounter. And, I might add, the only one worthy of your attention. Done correctly, with the stride of truth, you have everything to gain and nothing to lose.

To begin your journey, let's back up a moment and define entrepreneurship. "Just what is an entrepreneur anyway?" It probably conjures up a whole string of images for you: new ideas and inventions; freedom and individuality; creativity and opportunity. Success and riches are also usually envisioned. While not everyone who has an idea and follows through on it is going to achieve huge financial success, that *is* one of the goals of entrepreneurship as I am using it here. Given the right finesse of mind, you are capable of achieving riches beyond your wildest fantasies.

Entrepreneurship is not about being nice and comfortable or just a little better off. It is about soaring—leaping, dancing and playing your way through life. You are to start handling problems in a way that keeps you up instead of dragging you down, letting the mighty spirit of entrepreneurship take over in your life, instead of being driven along at less than what you could be. You will learn how to push yourself to the limit without feeling pushed. And as you are off and running, the harder you run, the stronger you will feel the wind blowing with you.

Successful entrepreneurship lies in feeling the pull of the universe rather than the push. It's not so much getting a kick in the seat of the pants like we are so often taught (because the law of gravity will quickly plop you right back down) as it is being drawn up, magnetically almost magically, into a success time frame.

Frequently, as the would-be entrepreneur forges out on his or her own, s/he makes the mistake of an acquaintance of mine, Larry. Larry couldn't wait to quit his job. He had a little money saved to tide him over and a bundle of ideas and interests.

Nevertheless, two years after leaving his place of employment, he woke up to find his money depleted and no profit in sight. Larry had spent long hours engrossed in a number of pet projects, learning many new things and enjoying a variety of experiences. Entrepreneurial success and riches, however, never materialized. He had become victim to the route of the dilettante and hobbyist. Until basic survival needs became an issue, money goals held no important place in his mind.

Larry's mistake was a common one. It is easy to get caught up in pursuing our interests and hobbies hoping that in the process we will somehow figure out a way to profit, but never fully coming to terms with the money goals in our planning. Make no mistake about it, the entrepreneurial stride is to *both* pursue a project which captivates your interest *and* firmly create in your mind the riches outcome.

So that you do not wind up like Larry, as a mere hobbyist, you need to confront a very basic question: "Why become a millionaire?" "Why make a lot of money?" The answer to this question appears to be so self-evident, no one asks it seriously. "Of course", you say, "We all want to make a lot of money and be millionaires". Not true. I, for one, didn't. Nor do most of the people I have spoken with. Certainly, we want to be well off.

And we have many general needs and wishes. We'd like a better house, a new car, a vacation in Hawaii, and we have desires for love and friendship. None of the things uppermost in our minds however usually cost a tremendous amount—unless it's oceanfront real estate. You feel that you can easily enough afford most of what you would like to have, if not right this minute, in the near future. Your goals are probably realistic enough and close enough at hand to you financially if you just continue along in your same habit patterns, going to work each day and doing things pretty much as always.

This is the middle-class syndrome. It is not true for the down and out. A sizable proportion of those who have made it on their own have at one time been reduced to dire circumstances, suffered a major crisis or lived under unusually harsh conditions. They did not find themselves in that comfort zone of the vast majority of us. Things were so bad, they were willing to try anything, even stake their last dollar on a chance to improve their situation. They had everything to gain and little to lose.

Few of us fall into this class. We are happy, or reasonably so. Things are not all that bad. We have much of what we want. Why *should* you take the risk of disrupting your present lifestyle to go out on a limb on your own? You'd like to have *more,* but you're not keen at all on taking the risk of sacrificing what you presently have, regardless of how little that might be relative to what you are capable of attaining. You have spent years attempting to save up for a down payment on a house or reduce your existing home mortgage; you have traded up on a car; you go out for dinner a few times a week; and you can afford to take a pleasant vacation every year or so.

Although you'd like to have a better house, better car and travel more, *you don't have anything that definite in mind to get you excited enough to do a whole lot about it.* What *are* you going to actually *do* with millions of dollars? If you are like most people, other than idle dreaming, you haven't thought much about it. I'm sure if someone handed you a million tomorrow, you'd figure it out and have a good time doing so. Short of winning a lottery or inheriting a fortune, however, that isn't the way the universe operates to make you rich. First, you need to know why and what for. Until you have cleared this up with yourself, spectacular wealth is always going to be just out of reach. The only exception to this might be if someone got you started along the right time habit patterns early in life.

Worse yet, the better educated you are, the more degrees you have, and the more intelligent you are, the tougher. If you are a thinker, always seeking explanations before you act, it's even more difficult. Questioning every possible move you make burns up time and energy. Remnants of the work ethic surfacing your mind with its sentiments of frugality, parsimony and guilt over a life of ease act as a further constraint on your activities toward wealth. "To obtain riches accidently as a by-product of some more noble goal is palatable enough" most of us argue, "but to set my sights on the achievement of riches per se is surely shallow, selfish and downright sinful." Is it? Before you can ever hope to become solidly positioned on the path to high success, the "whys" of being an entrepreneur-millionaire need to be definitely and unequivocally resolved.

To help you come to terms with the whys and what-fors of going on your own, let's take a closer look at the benefits of successful entrepreneurship and the resulting riches. As an entrepreneur you have the opportunity to regain control over your life and time. Your aim is to learn how to plan your personal time in such a way that you can live where you want to live, do what you enjoy most, and grow rich in the process. As an entrepreneur, you have the freedom to create the world of your choosing—to shape and mold the events in your days, months and years, just as you wish.

You are about to embark on a new adventure. To whet your appetite and boost you in this direction I want you to consider eleven benefits of getting and staying excited about your entrepreneurial journey. For the moment, don't think about reasons why you cannot: only dwell on what can and will be yours. For until you become totally sold on a different lifestyle, nothing much is going to happen. As you read the following pages about the riches of entrepreneurship, begin visualizing yourself as part of this world. Use your imagination and do a little dreaming. In order for it to become a reality, you need to live, breathe and feel rich every minute of the day.

The Riches of Entrepreneurship

(1)A wholesome, healthy environment

No longer tied to a job site, you can live where you want to live, in a setting and climate of fresh, smogfree air. As you desire, you can live high in majestic mountains to breathe cool, thin, invigorating air. You can have a home perched atop an ocean cliff and fall asleep to the crashing, soothing sounds of the waves. Or you might choose to live aboard a luxury yacht and sail the Pacific.

No longer must you endure the noise, congestion, traffic and fumes that set blood boiling and tempers flaring. You have the riches to seek out the geographical location and kind of environment just right for you, one that aligns with your personality, needs and interests.

(2)Scientific & technological innovations for your well-being

As a multi-millionaire, you have the purchasing power to take advantage of all the marvels of modern civilization. You can own your own private yacht and sail across the oceans. You can have a jet airplane with private pilot to take you where you want to go when you want to go. You can be a consumer of the finest technological innovations. Here is a sample list to stimulate your imagination:

(a)A quality stereo sound system that does not reek of static to grate on your nerves and raise your stress level.

(b)A video cassette player with the latest entertainment and educational films to enjoy in the privacy of your home.

(c)A home video camera to let you capture the special moments in the life of your loved ones and yourself.

(d)As a supplement to the presence of maids and servants, a computer robot is a wonderful creature to have around the house.

(e)The multi-uses of a word processor keeps your files organized and helps with correspondence.

(f)A computer system to speed through your business calculations and take care of bookkeeping for you.

(g)A library of disc data banks puts you instantly in touch with newspapers, magazines and other media around the world.

(h)Without leaving the beautiful, healthy surroundings of your home, and with the use of convenient computer technology, you can send and receive messages among friends, relatives, business associates or whomever you choose. If desired, you need never again subject yourself to traffic, crowds, noise and congestion.

The possibilities are endless!

(3)Educational advantages

With plenty of money available, see yourself taking advantage of the many informative seminars, workshops and conferences that are available. At your discretion you can attend those classes that correspond with your personal and entrepreneurial goals and objectives, traveling to the sites of your choice: Macau, Maui, Monterey. Or, make use of satellite to stay at home on your lanai overlooking the ocean to communicate with instructors and other students afar.

No longer must you spend time reading materials and attending meetings set by your employer to further a business which may be only remotely related to your own goals. Now, you are free to direct your energies toward the pursuit of those objectives which match your particular needs and interests.

In your quiet moments you can bask in the books, audio and video tapes of your choice, pursuing whatever new learning experiences your heart desires: eighteenth century literature, biographies of the great, or the latest marketing strategies.

(4)A more enjoyable fitness & health program

With money no longer a factor, you can join those health spas, tennis clubs, swim and recreation clubs with the finest facilities and coaches for superior health and well-being. Or you may elect to have your own private pool, suntan salon, tennis courts, putting greens and all the remarkable gym equipment that is currently available to make exercise a pleasure instead of a chore. Personal and mechanical masseuses will undoubtedly become a regular part of your daily and weekly routine.

(5)A safer environment

Prior to amassing a fortune, safety devices and helpmates are frequently the first things that get neglected. For your automobiles, safety assurances would include regular maintenance, tune-ups, good tires, quality seat belts, flashing light emergency signals, and snow tires or chains when necessary.

Home safety measures would include keeping your appliances in good working order and making certain that any heating fixtures, faulty wiring and other potential fire hazards are repaired promptly.

Depending on your location, a home burglary alarm system may be needed to alleviate crime, intrusions, and give greater peace of mind to yourself and family.

Safety equipment for your adult toys is a must. Your boat, airplane, cycle and other toys have expensive upkeep. A good radio and depth indicator for your yacht helps insure the safety of you and your passengers. A de-icer radar system for your airplane is a must in many areas.

When short on cash, all too often these are just the things we let slide, jeopardizing not only our own safety, but that of others.

(6)Better preventative & medical care

While your new riches give you the means for maintaining a more accident-free, stress-free and disease-free lifestyle, you will also have the peace of mind that comes from knowing you can afford the best medical care for yourself and loved ones should it become necessary.

(7)Greater aesthetic appeal of your surroundings

Though you may never have been an art collector or wish to spend a lot of time with your newfound wealth to shop for art objects, your immediate environment and surroundings of artifacts, different hues and textures has a definite impact on your mental and emotional state. You now have the option to make use of an interior designer and hire a personal shopping consultant. Work with an architect to draw up plans and build the kind of house you have always wanted. Hire a landscape artist to tailor your home grounds with greenery, fountains and flowers.

Everything about you has an influence on your disposition, your mood, and how you think and feel. With abundant wealth you are coming closer to having the power to create your own temperament and happiness.

(8)Gift giving without dollar remorse

Experience the joy of giving money and gifts to your family, friends, colleagues and those who have provided you with support and love. All too often we put ourselves in hock at Christmas time or for birthdays and special occasions, making purchases we cannot really afford. What a thrill to buy gifts and give generously out of your new surplus of dollars! What a thrill to feel good about giving! And what joy to not have to worry about running up credit card balances that never get fully paid!

(9)Financial support of worthwhile organizations and businesses

Freed from supporting yourself via a job, you will no

longer be in the uncomfortable financial position where you are directly or indirectly aiding those businesses whose products, services and operations are in discord with your value system. And once you have established a sound financial base of your own and have extra dollars on hand, you can lend monetary support to those associations, cultural institutions and fledgling enterprises that meet your ideals for the betterment of humankind. For example, these might be individuals and groups organized to wipe out poverty, reduce crime, assist the homeless, promote better communication, peace, a more stable economic system, a healthier environment or whatever you have a special interest in seeing improved.

(10)The upgrading of your own business enterprise

With additional funds, you can purchase all the latest office paraphernalia, expand your computer network, and hire the needed staff to attend to all the details of your new business while you give yourself free rein to those creative and challenging aspects of the business.

(11)Improved personal & social relationships

Insufficient money is a strain on any relationship. Financial problems and disputes are one of the biggest sources of friction between couples. Dining out, entertaining, taking trips together, giving each other gifts, and visiting romantic vistas around the globe all cost money. In modern society, the best things in life are definitely not free. Even sitting by the ocean watching a magnificent sunset does not come cheap if you happen to live a thousand miles away from such a site. Staying at home to watch video cassette tapes first requires purchasing or renting the equipment and films.

Whether you are single or married, there is a constant outflow of dollars in your social life for meals, beverages, excursions, places to visit and things to do. Even something as basic as pure, clean drinking water costs money in many locales. And as personal and free-sounding an activity as making love bears financial costs for birth control and all the human titillators we desire for our pleasure.

Extra leisure from a surplus of dollars will also give you more time to spend with your closest friends, family and sweetheart.

In short, with the riches of entrepreneurship, you can live where you want to live, do what you want to do and find greater happiness in all dimensions of your life.

You see then, becoming a successful entrepreneur encompasses much more than the accumulation of material possessions: owning a bigger house, buying a Ferrari, Gucchi bags and gold adornments. At stake is your very health, life and well-being. At stake is living in a clean, wholesome environment, your personal safety, having mind-expansion resources readily available, and the fostering of love and friendship. Best of all, as an entrepreneur, you have the peace of mind that can only come from taking charge of your time and working toward those goals and objectives you have set for yourself and that are in keeping with your value system and personal philosophy. Education takes on a new meaning in the world of the entrepreneur. Learning endeavors are no longer viewed with an eye toward getting a better, higher paying job, but as a process to discover and direct your creative energies toward the fulfillment of your mission in life. More and more persons today are finding that they cannot afford to deny themselves the riches of entrepreneurship. Can you?

It is imperative that you start setting the stage now, even before you finish reading this book. You can expand and correct as you go along. The toughest part is taking that first step and building up enough momentum to keep you going until you have figured out all the details of your new enterprise and begin reaping the benefits. At that point, your behavior patterns will become self-reinforcing and the amount of effort and energy required will level off. To get you over this initial hump, on the page that follows, take five minutes and write down all the personal benefits and rewards of being on your own. Use the above eleven categories of riches as a guide. What entices you the most? Your list will probably include tangible and intangible kinds of rewards: for example, a yacht on the Monterey Peninsula, a cozy cabin on lake Tahoe, traveling to new places, as well as the thrill of being on your own.

Time Block No. 1
Millionaire Play Sheet

Take five minutes *now* and list below the personal rewards and benefits of being on your own.

1.

2.

3.

4.

5.

6.

7.

8.

9.

10.

Thoughts on Prosperity & Poverty

To further motivate you toward the value of riches in your life, here are some thoughts on prosperity and poverty to ponder:

Michael Harrington.—"Those who suffer levels of life well below those that are possible, even though they live better than medieval knights or Asian peasants, are poor."

John Gardner.—"For every talent that poverty has stimulated it has blighted a hundred."

P. T. Barnum.—"Money is a terrible master but an excellent servant."

Albert Camus.—"It's a kind of spiritual snobbery that makes people think they can be happy without money."

Samuel Johnson.—"You never find people laboring to convince you that you may live very happily upon a plentiful income."

George Bernard Shaw.—"Very few people can afford to be poor."

Sophie Tucker.—"I've been rich and I've been poor; rich is better."

Maxim Gorky.—"With his(her) own money a person can live as he(she) likes..."

George Gissing.—"Money is time. With money I buy for cheerful use the hours which otherwise would not in any sense be mine; nay, which would make me their miserable bondsman."

W. Somerset Maugham.—"Money is like a sixth sense without which you cannot make a complete use of the other five."

Publilius Syrus.—"Money alone sets all the world in motion."

John D. Rockefeller.—""You will find money the best of friends—if not the best friend—you have."

Mark Twain.—"Some men worship rank, some worship heroes, some worship power, some worship God, and over these ideals they dispute—but they all worship money."

Samuel Johnson.—"It is better to live rich than to die rich."

George Bernard Shaw.—"Modern poverty is not the poverty that was blest in the Sermon on the Mount."

For many highly successful entrepreneurs, it is the challenge of building their own empire, whatever the field of endeavor, that keeps their juices flowing and their enthusiasm alive. They may have little interest in the adult consumer toys (cars, boats, vacations and gadgets) which they are able to purchase as fruits of their labor. The excitement is in the conquest of creating anew, overcoming obstacles, having an impact on their culture and environment or influencing the course of events. Still, for others, the prime motivator is not so much what money will buy but how much green stuff they can accumulate. It matters little to them that they, their family and heirs will never be able to spend it all; the thrill lies in building a financial network and seeing how much they can increase their net worth over the shortest period of time. Actually, many entrepreneurs are conservative in their expenditures. They are quick to sacrifice comfort and convenience to devote time to a project in which they believe.

Until you build up your own momentum as an entrepreneur, however, it is strongly urged that you come to terms with the value and rewards of money so as not to have any reservations about its acquisition. If you start off with mixed feelings about making a lot of money, have any guilt over its pursuit or an attitude that maybe you don't deserve much in life, this is going to kill your chances for success. Without a clear conscience, the first time you run into a problem or stumbling block, you are prone to start questioning whether you are doing the right thing, fall into conflict, procrastinate and lose the passion and single-minded purpose so essential to reaching the top.

Also, focusing on the rewards of riches, those items you truly want, helps to keep your energy level up when you are having a bad day or things aren't going as well as you would like.

In a later chapter you will learn about different kinds of prosperity props to keep your spirit soaring no matter what. For the moment, put the **Millionaire Play Sheet** you have just done in a conspicuous place at home and in the office so that you can refer to it often. Read it over out loud at least once a day.

To reach the heights of success as quickly as possible you need to know where you currently stand and begin charting your path. What attitudes, motivations and time-action patterns are bolstering your riches? What sorts of things are sabotaging your chances for abundant wealth? To help you assess your present entrepreneurial status, take the quiz on the next page. It is designed to give you insights on the changes you want to begin incorporating into your life.

Rate yourself next to each of the statements according to the scale. Don't dwell long on any one question. The logic behind some of the statements may not be completely clear to you at this point, however, it will become better understood as we go along. The quiz should take you about fifteen minutes to complete. Do this now. If a particular statement does not apply to you, respond as though you were in such a situation. Be honest!

Time Block No. 2
Entrepreneur Quiz

Rate yourself on each of the thirty questions below according to the scale.

1 Almost never
2 Rarely
3 Occasionally
4 Fairly often
5 Almost always

(1)In my daily lifestyle I maintain a clear sense of purpose and direction.
(2)I enjoy scheduling my own time blocks and working on my own.
(3)I act with courage in the face of uncertainty without being overly concerned about making mistakes.
(4)I am action-oriented and unlikely to put off those things that I can do today.
(5)I trust my own judgment and avoid leaning excessively on others to make my decisions or assure me it is okay to go ahead.

(6)I act and correct for my mistakes immediately as new information and feedback becomes available.
(7)I allocate my time in accordance with the priority goals in my life.
(8)I have high powers of concentration and refuse to let distractions get in the way.
(9)When talking with others about my business ventures, I stick to the point, always keeping in mind my end goal.
(10)In obtaining information from others, my questions are direct and consistent with my objectives.

(11)I am likely to find myself thoroughly immersed in my business projects, in a way that my consciousness is totally consumed by the task at hand.
(12)Even when I am at rest, I find my self-talk is related to my enterprises.
(13)My self-talk is positive, finding opportunities in problems and obstacles.
(14)I delight in a good challenge, however don't consider myself to be a big gambler.
(15)I have set short term objectives as well as long term goals for greater achievement and success.

(16)My enterprise goals have been well-formulated and are clear and specific.
(17)When I become involved in something I stay with it to its completion.
(18)I objectively analyze past mistakes to improve my performance in the future.
(19)When I decide to do something, I find a way to do it.
(20)I am excited and enthused about the work I have chosen.

(21)I listen carefully when someone gives me feedback on my projects.
(22)I have a strong vision of how my product or service is beneficial in the marketplace.
(23)I act consistently to turn my dreams into a reality.
(24)Even when I'm tired, I find it easy to work toward my goals.
(25)I refrain from eating, drinking and smoking excessively.

(26)Exercise or some physical activity is a regular part of my day.
(27)In the face of uncertainty, I act as if a successful outcome is imminent.
(28)In my dealings with others, I harbor no malice, ill-will or resentment.
(29)When in doubt, I avoid wasting time pondering and procrastinating but act...then correct as I go along.
(30)I apply a consistent business philosophy and act in accordance with my own value system, with integrity and honesty.

Bravo. You have taken a crucial step toward riches. Add up your points to see what your present rating is. 130 or more is outstanding; 115 to 129 is excellent; 100 to 114 is good.

Do not be disappointed if you scored low at this time because that is rapidly going to change. On the other hand, if you are one of the few to score high, congratulations! You are going to go further than you have imagined in your wildest dreams.

Let's summarize some of these key characteristics of the successful entrepreneur so that you can start seeing yourself in this image.

Most important of all is the ability to take charge of your time. As a successful entrepreneur you know how to use your time effectively. You do not waste time. The minutes of the day are held in high esteem, as golden nuggets. You have a clear perspective about where you are going and time is focused toward your goals, not only long term goals, but three month goals, one month goals, and weekly objectives. Each day is viewed as a new adventure in time, awaiting the impact of your creative touch to bring about those changes for the betterment of yourself and humanity.

As a successful entrepreneur, you have a single-minded purpose and are not scattered in your thinking and action. Unlike a dilettante that flitters from one activity to another, you adhere to the motto, "Do one thing at a time and do it well".

You have the courage to take calculated risks. While successful entrepreneurs are rarely compulsive gamblers, they have the self-confidence to act in the face of uncertainty, make a decision and stick with it. You cannot sit on the fence and get ahead.

A dominant quality is perseverance. You have that unique ability to keep your eye on the goal and stay with it *in spite of* whatever comes up and gets in the way. Failure is not a word in your vocabulary.

Entrepreneurs are opportunity-minded. You keep an open mind for new ideas and ways of doing things. Instead of seeing problems, you see solutions and opportunities all about you.

You care about others. As a successful entrepreneur you take a genuine interest in others' welfare, and look for product improvements and services to fill a need in the marketplace. Petty politics, resentment and envy have no place in your day.

You are a good listener. Without letting your ego get in the way, you take into account comments, criticism and feedback from others. When appropriate, you solicit information on how you can better perform your services and functions.

You have high standards of integrity and honesty. You have thought through a sound personal philosophy and act in accordance with your own value system, constantly striving to fulfill meaningful, worthwhile goals.

Finally, you take that extra step toward excellence, living by the motto: "I will do my best, and then a little more."

Time Block No. 3
Entrepreneur Affirmations

Each of the ideas in the quiz you have just taken represents an affirmation which needs to become a habitual part of your life. To innervate you in this direction, underline and star those affirmations on which you rated yourself "fairly often" or "almost always". Assure their reinforcement in your life by repeating them once each morning when you first awaken and again at night before you drift off to sleep.

Now, go back over the list and circle the remainder of the affirmations where you rated yourself "1" almost never, "2" rarely or "3" occasionally. With these you need extra practice before they are fully a part of your action patterns. Ingrained habit patterns are adamant to change and a long time in reversing unless you make use of the appropriate catalysts.

Begin chipping away any faulty habits by giving your undivided attention to the positive patterns. Avoid dwelling on what you've been doing wrong and beating yourself over the head. The shortcomings in your daily routine will easily slip away, unmissed and unnoticed as your success time habits expand. *Energy follows thought.* Therefore, all your thoughts, images, feelings, sentiments and action tendencies need to be bombarded with success postures and nothing else. You want to allow no space whatsoever in your day for doubt, negative judgments or anything else likely to lead you off course.

Relentless repetition of the starred affirmations is your first task to reverse the flow of energy back where it should be. Along with reinforcing your strengths through daily reading each morning and night, you are to block out ten minutes to state out loud, over and over, the affirmations you have just circled. That's approximately thirty minutes a day total you are to be spending toward riches. As we progress, you will learn to block out more and more time, until eventually every minute of the day is in some way impacting on your wealth.

What you are discovering is how to set up each area of your life in a manner that perpetuates your entrepreneurial goals. This includes the physical plane, the cognitive plane and the affective plane of existence. The physical plane has to do with meeting those health, fitness and diet programs which provide you with a clear head for making business decisions, abundant energy to carry you through long days without feeling fatigue or discouragement and keep you free of debilitating disease.

The cognitive or mental plane of existence makes use of your imagination to create those symbols and images conducive to entrepreneurial riches. For example, you want to automatically start thinking of yourself as decisive, successful and a high achiever. You need to easily form images of yourself as confident and capable of handling whatever challenge presents itself.

The affective realm, in contrast, has to do with your desire: it is the torch for your riches, and the focal point of this book. It is the fire and passion for your behavior. Without it you are destined to be less than your best. Throughout the book you will be introduced to a variety of strategies and processes to keep this flame alive. You want your dominant thoughts, feelings and images to center around exactly those events in your life which you wish to happen. And happen they will, just as surely as the sun glistens across the Hawaiian Islands.

The Entrepreneurial Challenge On-Going Time Blocks

Time Block No. 1 Millionaire Play Sheet

Spend five minutes each evening before drifting off to sleep reading out loud the list of personal rewards and benefits of being on your own which you compiled.

Time Block No. 3 Entrepreneur Affirmations

Spend five minutes each morning and five minutes each evening repeating the affirmations that you have starred.

Spend ten minutes each evening repeating over and over the affirmations that you have circled.

Block these times out in your calendar now!

11
How to Play your Way to Prosperity

"Poverty is an anomaly to rich people; it is very difficult to make out why people who want dinner do not ring the bell."

—Walter Bagehot

3
Solving Cash Flow

"My life is a bubble; but how much solid cash it costs to keep that bubble floating!"

—LOGAN PEARSALL SMITH

Until you are fully underway and money begins to come in from your entrepreneurial projects, you will need to have a source of income to cover the costs of your living expenses. This could be from a return on investments, wages from temporary employment, obtaining a loan or some combination of these. Basically, you want to set yourself up with enough capital and income so that you have the peace of mind to pursue your entrepreneurial goals without the burden of financial need hanging over your head.

It is absolutely imperative that the time allotted for your personal projects be free of anxiety, fear and worry. For this reason, it is not recommended that you go heavily into debt to fund your projects with no other source of income. While it is true that many products and services have been borne out of financial necessity, it is also true that a greater number of new business enterprises have gone under due to insufficient capital. In any case, the aim here is to show you how to arrange your time space in a manner that is free from both internal and external constraints so that your creative self can go all out for you. You want to have the peace of mind and security to play around with your ideas and turn them into a profit, not clutter up your head with unpaid bills.

To help you toward this end, there are three preliminary measures to take prior to quitting work and plunging into entrepreneurship:

(A)Target any investment income you currently have available;

(B)Assess whether your consumer habit patterns and expenditures can be improved upon;

(C)Take temporary or part time employment to tide you over until your business is established.

Since few of us have sufficient investment capital and income to carry us for any length of time, the major portion of this chapter is devoted to the problem of getting set up with temporary work that will interfere as little as possible with your entrepreneurial objectives.

Investment income

Although this is not a book about how to make investments or get the best return on your dollar, you need to take a critical look at any capital which you currently have available and determine whether it is relatively secure and earning a reasonable rate of return. This is especially a must if you are counting on the money from your investments to hold you over until your enterprise is profit-producing.

The difficulty lies in ascertaining just what constitutes a secure investment, and what can be called a reasonable rate of return. The key variable to attend to in your financial choices is *change:* ongoing changes in economic factors, in the political arena and in the psychological domain. Of these, keeping abreast of changes in the psychological sphere is the most crucial for safeguarding and multiplying your investments. The greater your predictive power here, the better. If you can anticipate what others are about to do, you will always be one step ahead regardless of the type investment you hold or are interested in acquiring. Therefore, be continually alert to shifts of thinking that might affect your investments. If you observe that people are losing confidence in our banking system, for example, this may no longer be a safe place to put your money. Recognize, however, that there is no such thing as a permanent or 100% secure investment. And a so-called secure investment today may be folly tomorrow.

Even if you are in a position to hire a financial manager, I strongly urge you to stay on top of your money yourself. At least have a working knowledge of what's going on generally in the investment world and in particular where your dollars are concerned. Remember, when it comes to your money, you and only you, have the most at stake to gain or lose. Don't expect the experts to figure everything out for you and protect you.

Criteria for arriving at a reasonable rate of return on your dollars means looking to the marketplace. While a twelve per cent rate of return looks good at this writing, next year seven per cent or fifteen per cent may be reasonable. As a rule of thumb, the higher the rate of return, the greater the risk, however, there are many exceptions to this. With good information and first-hand knowledge, risk decreases. This does *not* mean relying on tips.

Usually, the best you can hope for is security in terms of your own state of mind. That is, you want to select those investment sources where you personally feel the most comfortable and are free from undue anxieties over possible losses. This is going to depend mostly on your own personality and past investment history. Whether you decide to play the options market or put your money in the more conservative money market accounts is a matter of personal taste and know-how. Three general guidelines for making investments are:

(1)Invest in those areas in which you are most familiar.

(2)Educate yourself in investment possibilities that arouse your interest and look promising. This can be accomplished through reading, talking with financial planners and attending investment seminars.

(3)Block out regular times during the week to better inform yourself, narrow your investment alternatives and follow through. More will be said on how to go about doing this shortly. Most of the hours of the day are to be earmarked for your new enterprise. Expect to spend a fairly small amount of time setting up and maintaining your investments. Your aim is to pave the way for your entrepreneurial mode of being and avoid getting encumbered with too many details and complications elsewhere.

Consumer choices

Another area within your control is your consumer expenditures. Wise purchases put dollars in your pocket toward your new business start up. First, consider any current expenses that you can cut out or cut back on. For instance, it could be the expensive apartment rental, the Porsche with its high monthly payments and heavy insurance premiums, or entertainment and dining out excessively. Thoreau has wisely observed, "The true cost of anything in life... is the part of your life you are willing to exchange." It is not just a question of whether you value the Porsche, the expensive wardrobe or other amenities, but the personal cost you are willing to pay.

Often when we are caught up in full time work and all its related off-the-job activities, we make poor consumer choices. We buy items on the run that we don't need and sometimes never even use. If you are like most people, you have shoes, shirts, slacks and other clothes stashed away in the closet that have barely been worn. On the work treadmill, we get in a hurry and overpay for food, apparel and other items instead of checking the market for lower prices as well as better quality. For major purchases, such as a car, too many of us buy on impulse and wind up with a lemon that turns out to be one repair bill after another. And stuck in a job you dislike, you are likely spending more to support bad habits such as over-eating, smoking and drinking.

Scrutinize your consumer expenditures, current needs, and consider changes to make. A word of caution: don't go overboard and try to cut out all your recreational and pleasure expenses. Simply take a realistic look at your present lifestyle and how your consumer expenditures stack up against the benefits realized.

Begin to evaluate your purchases in terms of the hours, weeks or months you put in to pay for them. Get in the habit of asking yourself, "Is this really what I want? Is it worth the time and labor cost?" Two major items you will want to examine are housing and automobile. How much of your work time goes toward producing income to meet the mortgage payments or rent on your home? How many months a year are you working at an unsatisfying job to meet the payments, expenses and maintenance on your automobiles? What are some alternatives to reduce your costs? Several possibilities are provided below:

Housing.

(1)Share an apartment with a friend or get a housemate. This style of living is becoming increasingly popular, especially in desirable locations where the cost of housing is expensive. California coastal regions, the Hawaiian Islands, Westchester County, New York and parts of Connecticut are prime examples. Formerly this style of living was only seen among men and women under thirty, now we see people of all ages sharing housing for both cost and companionship reasons.

(2)Seek a smaller, less expensive home or apartment. A little paint and imagination can do wonders for the lower-priced fixer-upper rentals.

(3)Get a rent reduction. Be aware that landlords and landladies *love* tenants who do not call them for every little repair. If you pay your rent on time and can guarantee your landlord that you will only bother him or her for major repairs, you probably can negotiate a rent reduction. Another way to get reduced rent is by paying several months rent in advance. All landlords are not rich and many will be delighted to give you a break on the rent for advance payment. If you live in an apartment building with a number of other tenants, keeping an eye out for vandalism or doing odd jobs such as gardening and repairs can also result in a rent reduction from landlords. Get in the habit of thinking in terms of the landlord's needs and you'll find yourself showered with benefits of lower rent and no rental increases.

(4)Go in together with another family or a friend to purchase a home. Or buy a house that has separate guest quarters and rent this space out to keep your monthly payments down. As housing costs climb, we are seeing a heightened interest in duplexes and residential homes with separate units.

Transportation.

In our modern society, we have been so conditioned to the notion of private automobile ownership, few of us seriously consider what else we might do to solve our transportation problems. Actually, there are many viable and superior alternatives. Since the cost and expenses associated with car ownership eat up such an enormous chunk of your work year, I am going to elaborate on this at some length.

If you paid $10,000 for your automobile, financed it at twelve per cent over four years and are earning $500 per week for a forty hour week, in effect you are putting in roughly *4 months a year of your time on the job to pay for your auto.* This is without taking into account the expenses of insurance, registration, license plates, gasoline, oil and maintenance, and parking or traffic tickets. If you are working at a job you dislike, four+ months is a lot of time. What else could you be doing with this one-third of a year? Is the car worth it?

"But, what choice do I have?" I'm sure you are protesting. "I can't live without a car (or cars). I have to drive to work, to the grocer's, shopping, run errands, go to meetings, social affairs, ad infinitum. And what about outings, traveling across state and to the beach?" Unpleasant visions of riding on a crowded public bus and waiting on the street corner for taxis flash before your eyes.

Buses and subways aside, there are a variety of ways to solve your transportation needs. For weekend outings you can lease a car, perhaps even a newer and better one than you are presently driving. Many people do this already. On other occasions, for shopping, errands and evening engagements, you can take taxis and occasionally even a chic stretch limo with private chauffeur. Taking taxis and limos may sound extravagant, however, did you know that for less than half the cost of the average-price automobile of $10,000, you can take twelve 3-hour limousine trips with a private chauffeur, rent a new car for twenty weekends and take *one hundred* taxi rides at $12 each? Contrary to what most of us assume, being without a car and taking advantage of different alternatives can spell greater luxury for less cost.

More likely than the costs, private automobile ownership for most folks is tied up with their ego and image. Thanks to the millions of advertising dollars spent by the automobile industry, we have come to see ourselves as someone who drives a Chevy or Toyota or Mercedes. The cars we own have become part of our identity. To help you car de-condition yourself, did you know that there are dozens of millionaires, celebrities and prominent persons who *choose* to be without car ownership? And many, many upper-income executives and ordinary people in urban cities such as New York and San Francisco have gotten rid of their cars. This may surprise you but *private automobile ownership is rapidly on the way to becoming obsolete.*

Some of the individual and societal benefits of not owning a car are listed below:

No parking hassles. A taxi or limousine takes you exactly where you want to go. No more driving around and around the block searching futilely for parking places that do not exist.

Greater safety from muggings. Being required to park six blocks or more away from your friend's house, for dinner at a restaurant or social meeting and walking back to your car late at night in many areas is just plain unsafe. Having a taxi pick you up at the door of your evening engagement makes sense.

More safety from accidents. A substantial number of people put off keeping their private autos in the best of repair and well-maintained. Many of us postpone buying new tires when we need them and making other repairs that pose safety hazards on the road.

Save time. Most of us think that having a car in the garage at our immediate disposal to jump in and go some place saves time. But think again. Though you may need to wait for a taxi occasionally, you'll save time in a multitude of other ways without car ownership: No more waiting at DMV for registration, licenses and getting smog permits. No more taking your car in for an oil change, pumping gas or waiting at the service station. Gone is the task of searching for auto parts, having spark plugs changed, attempting to find a reputable maintenance shop and waiting for repairs.

You will also save time through consolidation of chores. Instead of jumping into the car every time you run out of a loaf of bread, if you are using a taxi you are going to plan ahead more and consolidate your errands, grocery shopping and other chores. This has the effect of saving both time and expense.

Be more physically fit. If no car is parked conveniently in your garage, you are automatically going to walk and bike more. Some of us have gotten so spoiled and soft we even "walk our dogs" in the car! Getting rid of our automobiles is the best thing that could happen to most of us.

Less pollution. While there will still be pollution from buses, taxis and limos, my guess is that consolidating our trips is going to cut down considerably on the number of vehicles on the highways.

Fewer inebriated drivers on the road. Organizations such as MADD have done much to promote public awareness concerning this issue. We know that over fifty per cent of serious accidents are related to drinking, yet few people have altered their lifestyle. When we own a car, we drive to a restaurant or a friend's house for dinner, have a couple drinks and drive home. Some of us may drink less if we are behind the wheel and this has helped, but the problem is nowhere close to being adequately solved. Hundreds of lives are lost each year and thousands more people are permanently maimed due to drinking and driving. Only when a substantial number of us give up automobile ownership will we begin to correct this problem.

Drive a better car. On weekends when you want to go on an outing or take a long trip, renting a car can be a lot of fun. You have a variety of different cars to choose from, often a newer, brighter and better model car than the one you formerly owned. Occasionally you can rent a Rolls Royce, Mercedes Benz, a Cadillac or whatever your personal preference. You'll have the opportunity of driving automobiles you may never have considered buying because of the cost.

To further dispel auto ownership conditioning, and rid yourself of this obsolete status symbol, here are some ideas on what to tell your friends when you sell your car:

(A)I decided to pamper myself and take chauffeur-driven limos instead.

(B)I lease a different new car on weekends when I need it and during the week I take taxis.

(C)I got tired driving the same color car for a whole year. Now I can rent a bright red one if that's what I'm in the mood for, or sapphire blue, silver or whatever I feel like.

(D)I like having someone else do the driving and being chauffeured around.

(E)I got tired of the parking hassle and driving in congestion.

(F)I'm saving money and living better.

Taking taxis and chauffeur-driven limousines around town to do your errands may sound unusual to you and not fit the current image you have of yourself. As a soon-to-be prosperous entrepreneur, however, this is an image you need to start cultivating. The sooner you begin thinking of yourself as going first class, the sooner it will happen.

In addition to re-evaluating your housing and automobile expenditures, check out your other consumer habits. You might want to take a vacation closer to home and cut out travel costs which can be set aside for your entrepreneurial budget. Examine your daily, weekly and monthly expenditure patterns. For example, many women are in the habit of going to the hairdresser every week even when they don't really feel like it. This could be changed to twice monthly with a substantial dollar savings. Put your mind to it and you will be surprised at how many things you come up with that you're spending money on but don't enjoy that much.

You know your financial situation best and with a little creative thought will easily be able to temporarily cut out or cut back on some of your expenditures to allow less financial stress and more time for your entrepreneurial quest. In economizing, begin to think in terms of your values and desires. On many occasions, you can cut expenses on items that you never really wanted or used in the first place. Reappraising what you genuinely like and want will go a long way toward eliminating costs and putting dollars in your pocket for your entrepreneurial pursuits.

Temporary employment

Until your personal projects begin paying off, and assuming that you are not lucky enough to have sufficient investment income to carry you, you will need to continue working for someone else. It is important to set yourself up with a job that is going to interfere as little as possible with your freedom and entrepreneurial objectives. The kind of work to seek from an entrepreneurial vantage point is in many respects the antithesis of what you have always been taught. We look now at seven of these new employment yardsticks. As you will see, they represent a radical departure from the usual job search. Whether it is time to quit your present job can also be more realistically assessed in view of these criteria.

(1)An occupation that requires little or no thought.

You do not want an occupation that is going to weigh on your mind and consume your consciousness. Your mind needs to be free to play around with the entrepreneurial goals you are laying out for yourself. This is where your priorities lie. Highly desirable work would be those "mindless jobs" that can be done while your thoughts are free to roam at will. Positions which we usually think of as falling into this class are such tasks as routine housework, physical labor and assembly line work. Today many mindless positions have opened up in computer-related fields. Although such work is denigrated today, these will be just the coveted and sought after, part-time jobs of the future when we want to put our minds at rest from the demanding, creative involvements of our own personal undertakings. As we evolve into a full scale society of entrepreneurs, taking a "work break" will mean taking time off from our own individual pursuits.

All you need be concerned about is your *intention* in filling these so-called menial work slots, so that your identity and self-worth do not get tied up and suffer the consequences. You have a higher purpose as an entrepreneur. Let the unenlightened diehard working class continue to drudge along looking for the mythical self-fulfilling occupation and give their best time and best shot to a firm whose goals only minimally match up with their own values, interests and objectives.

A growing number of individuals making up today's leisure ethic have already figured this out, shifted their thinking and are acting accordingly. We see physicists, accountants, corporate executives. secretaries and people from all walks of life who have left behind the high-paying, "prestige" positions to regain control over their own time and pursue their own thing. During the transition, jobs are being sought out which are nondemanding and require little thought or imagination. These are taken on as both an income supplement and as a diversion from more important personal projects.

In other instances, "low-level" jobs are taken up as an investigative experience. A mathematics professor at the University of Hawaii had a lifelong dream of owning and operating an Italian restaurant. In order to begin fulfilling his ambitions in this direction, he decided to learn the business from the bottom up. Scanning the help-wanted ads in the local newspaper, he spotted an ad for a part-time busboy at a nearby Italian restaurant. He applied for the job and started work. Clear about what he wanted, this "low status" position turned out to be fun, rewarding and a learning experience consistent with his entrepreneurial goals. Frank is now the proud owner of not one, but three highly successful restaurants.

Jerri, a novelist, tells how she worked as a file clerk at several different businesses to gather material for her latest book, and as a respite from the creative thinking required in her life's work.

Another woman, Karen, who has a masters degree in education, confessed to me how much she loved doing real estate deals. Taking a temporary job as an office clerk with a bustling real estate firm, she set out to learn every aspect of the business. For six weeks in between answering the telephone, she carefully observed investors come and go, who the movers and shakers were and what strategies were the most successful. Today, two years later after making investments on her own, her net worth has increased well over one million dollars.

Dan, a young ambitious financial whiz, relayed how he took a job as a bank teller until he got his own financial services business off the ground.

As I am sure you will recognize, what I am talking about in these examples is entirely different from the bright, overqualified person who takes a mindless job out of necessity rather than choice. This is a sure route to the work identity crisis we hear so much about. As long as your identity is locked into the occupation and position you hold, you are going to be subject to the occupational hazard of lowered self-esteem. Only when the value of your personal and entrepreneurial goals takes precedence and a time map for their completion is charted, will you be able to squelch the damaging self-image triggered by the occupational syndrome: the job search and rejection, the promotion you didn't get or an unexpected lay-off. Small wonder so many of us bury ourselves in mesmerizing after-work activities of booze and bondage to assuage our bruised egos and image!

(2)An occupation that requires as little time as possible.

Unless there is an eighty per cent or more alignment between your employer's goals and your own goals, you do not want to put in any more hours than necessary on the job. Look for a firm where you will have some control over the hours when you must be on site in the work setting. Also explore the growing number of positions in which you can work out of your home. These are currently available in the computer technology industry and through many of the more progressively managed firms. This has the added benefit of saving commute time.

Seek out work positions offering a measure of discretion and control over the hours committed to your employer so that when something comes up on your personal projects, you have flexibility. For instance, you might need to leave the work site for an hour and meet with an important client. A firm with flextime where you can choose when you start and stop work will give you more leeway in scheduling activities related to your own projects. If you have sufficient income from your investments, take a part-time job that requires less than twenty hours work per week. Making arrangements to time share with another person is one possibility. A number of firms permit two or more people to hold one full-time position. When you want to take time off, someone else is available to fill in for you.

Another promising work structure we are seeing more of is through independent work contracting to firms. In these situations you are renting or selling your time and expertise to a business. This is commonly done by teams of management consultants, however, for specific and specialized tasks outside of the work setting, contracting is becoming increasingly accepted by industry. This offers you the greatest flexibility of all.

The major requirement of any job you take, unless it is somehow helpful in your entrepreneurial goals, is that you have freedom to devote to your own projects. Be clear with yourself about your priorities: your employer's goals are to be subjugated to your personal objectives, not vice versa. Your loyalty, always remember, is to your own value system—no one else's.

(3)A work setting with minimal responsibility.

Avoid taking a position in a work setting with heavy demands and responsibilities where the daily pressures sap your energy, leaving you feeling drained and enervated. Nor do you want to commit yourself to any kind of occupation with tension-provoking duties that spill over into nonwork hours to make you irritable and nervous. Stay away from employment which you are mentally and emotionally likely to take home with you and that cuts into your personal time and well-being.

Strive to structure your work patterns in such a way that your peak energy level and creative best occur during time off rather than on employment time. With this in mind, whenever possible, plan to work at a job during those hours of the morning, afternoon or evening when you are mentally fatigued, saving your most alert hours for yourself. For instance, if you wake up at nine o'clock Monday morning tired and run-down from a late night before, go in and do your routine work stint then. Later in the day take a nap, shower or do a meditation relaxation exercise and get into your own projects after you are rested.

Our past work ethic mentality has indoctrinated and hampered us to such an extent that we unquestioningly do just the opposite. Regardless of how far removed our employer's goals may be from our own values and objectives, we give our best shot of performance within the work setting, subordinating our own projects to a time of day when we are mentally and physically exhausted. It's hardly surprising so many of us feel frustrated, in despair and have difficulty following through on the things that are vital in our lives! Until you succeed in dumping this superior work attitude baggage and putting your attention where it counts—on your personal projects—you are going to fall short of success and happy living.

(4)An occupation that lets you fill up paid work hours with your own projects.

Employers love me for this one! I'll address that issue in a minute. For yourself, look for those types of jobs and positions which give you the greatest leeway in doing your own projects while getting paid. Some examples would be in working as a receptionist, as a desk clerk or a telephone operator during a slack time of day or year. It might be doing the graveyard shift at a small hotel or being on duty during off-season at a resort. One enterprising motel night manager brainstormed during his quiet hours at the motel where he worked and came up with ideas for opening a successful appliance store. He and his partner now have a lucrative chain of appliance stores on the Monterey Peninsula in California.

Educational settings also offer several possibilities. For an agreed-upon fee, fill in for instructors when they need to have films shown, exams given or other situations where a live body is required but little mental activity. During this time, you can organize material on your project, do bookkeeping for yourself, read up on a pertinent topic or just do some creative thinking about your endeavors.

On the other side of the fence, check out those job opportunities where you have the authority to turn over a period of your work time to someone else while you go about your own business interests. College professors and lecturers frequently do this by having guest speakers take over their classes. Some years ago when I was an instructor at the University of Hawaii, I made arrangements with a colleague to cover my classes for a week while I explored real estate investments in San Francisco. My students in the psychology courses I was teaching were delighted to be exposed to a different point of view. My colleague enjoyed the challenge of teaching a new class and was pleased with the gift I brought her back to show my appreciation. Everyone benefited.

Other opportunities are found in those fields where you are "on call" and paid a salary but not required to work until a particular need presents itself. In the past, such types of positions were limited to only a few specialized professions, such as the medical and dental fields. Physicians, nurses, therapists and other personnel employed by hospitals are often able to remain at home or wherever they choose within a certain geographical radius and be paid while they are "on call" should their services be needed. More recently, this work concept has branched out to a myriad of other fields. In the law enforcement sector, scores of policemen, sheriffs and highway patrolmen stand by to meet a community need. Our era of technology and communications has opened up on-call positions for telephone operators, answering service personnel, and management at all levels. Possibilities exist in the tourist industry, financial services, and publishing fields.

If you are employed now, in many cases you can make the changes in your present job to free up more time for yourself. Accomplish this with the help of a supervisor, co-worker, or by doing a little creative rescheduling of meetings, clients and work tasks yourself. Every job offers some room for personal time flexibility. It is up to you to determine how much leeway your present occupation affords or whether you should switch to another "more promising" occupation.

(5)A temporary job that has an advantageous location.

Factors to take into consideration are: distance from home, the section of town, form of transportation to get to and from work and work-related travel. How much commuting time will you need to spend? Are you going to be spending thirty minutes a day or two hours? Is the mode of transportation mostly by private automobile, taxi, bus, train, ferry boat or airplane? A long commute to and from work is not necessarily a drawback if you can carry out activities pertinent to your business enterprise en route. For instance, on a plane trip you can catch up on correspondence, make telephone calls, dictate proposals and listen to cassette tapes. Many of these same business activities can be accomplished in a long automobile drive provided there is little traffic. A two hour highway drive in light traffic is quite different from the same time spent in heavy urban traffic congestion with a lot of starts and stops and hot-tempered drivers. In reviewing a potential job prospect, take into account the section of town or suburbs you must commute through. How much congestion, pollution and noise must you contend with? Breathing exhaust fumes and dealing with short-tempered motorists for two hours or more, day-in and day-out, is no way to spend your time.

Assess the location of your temporary job according to its convenience in relation to your entrepreneurial projects and investments. Let's say your main source of investment income is from rental property that you have purchased in a certain area and you are managing the apartments yourself. You probably would not want to take a position requiring extensive out-of-town travel. And commuting to work by taxi, train or car pool would be preferable to driving in order to give yourself time to do the paperwork on your real estate transactions. It would also be desirable to have your place of temporary employment in the same general vicinity as your rental properties to more easily keep an eye on them. The same holds true for many other types of personal investments and businesses.

In other words, your frame of reference in deciding on a temporary job site should always fall back on whether it makes sense from the standpoint of your entrepreneurial and investment objectives.

(6)A work-site with harmonious interpersonal relationships.

Typically when you accept a new job, you walk into a ready-made social structure of supervisors, co-workers, and subordinates. Every social milieu has a certain emotional climate about it of which you want to take note. If the interpersonal relationships are disharmonious and it looks like you will be caught in a setting strewn with bad tempers, resentments, hostilities and petty office politics, think twice before going to work there. Such an environment cannot help but impact on you and be disruptive to your state of mind. You want your consciousness to be free and focused on your life enterprise, not burdened with the need to continually purge itself of ill chatter.

Although an office's emotional climate is by no means an easy thing to determine in advance, asking a lot of questions before you commit to starting work will help. Talk with the people in the department where you are going to be working. Observe the interactions of those about you and their degree of openness, warmth and friendliness. Staying aware of your personal objectives during the job interview is a step in this direction.

(7)A physical work setting conducive to your well-being.

A final occupational characteristic to broach is the physical environment at your prospective place of employment. Is it subject to glaring neon lights, smoke and pollution? Are you going to have to contend with irritating noises—clicking word processors and computer bells, noisy printers and nostalgic music?

How much work space will you have? Are your needs for sufficient personal space and peace of mind going to be met?

Problems such as this can drain you both mentally and physically, leaving you feeling down and out by the end of the day, a state of mind anathema to going home and bouncing enthusiastically and energetically into your own projects.

In sum, you want to seek out those temporary work positions that take up as little time, consciousness, and thought as possible. Preferably you will have flexible hours, be in an advantageous location, have harmonious social surroundings, and an aesthetically pleasing, healthy working environment. Ideally there will be no big conflicts between your functions at work and your personal value system.

Now, it is most unlikely that you are going to find the perfect temporary job as I have just described it anymore than you have been able to find the mythical, self-fulfilling career. The main consideration in tabulating the above standards is to assist you in pinpointing a whole new set of job criteria that make sense from your entrepreneurial stance. The closer you come to freeing yourself from job obligations and tasks which are in discord with your entrepreneurial interests and goals, the quicker you are going to spiral to success.

Another important point to make here is that the above job criteria are not to be construed in any way as license to take advantage of your employer by approaching your temporary position in a slovenly manner or being irresponsible to your work assignments. In accepting employment, for whatever paltry salary or distasteful duties, you have nonetheless contracted to provide a service to the best of your ability. What you are seeking in a temporary position is not an excuse to smirch your work responsibilities or do an injustice to your employer, but flexible employment arrangements that are consistent with your own personal goals and objectives.

Far from shunning your responsibility to others, you are assuming a much larger role in society as an entrepreneur. From this new vantage point you are shifting the locus of control and decision-making back to where it belongs, i.e., your own value system, rather than turning it over to someone else and, in effect, making decisions by default. Your entrepreneurial mission is based on more than economic gain and personal pleasure motives. It is an expression of who you are and your authenticity on this planet.

Instead of operating from the periphery of existence by shoving your personal values and goals into the background, you are putting your world together in a form that bears the highest burden of social responsibility and choice. The mark you make in the world will be a product of your own hands and heart. There is to be no more hiding behind the mask of "having done one's duty, service and job" simply because we have lived out our days faithfully putting in time for some corporation, government body or other employer. The integrity of such a stance has always been questionable, as was so dramatically illustrated in the 1960's, but the time was not yet ripe for individual entrepreneuring success on a massive world scale. The lingering uneasiness and frustration of these earlier years has remained, waiting for our evolution and the scientific and technological developments to bail us out of our predicament—this time with renewed vigor toward material prosperity as well as spiritual amity. The twenty-first century holds this promise for each of us.

In future days, our present dominant business and government systems will recede into the background, being mere shadows of an industrial past. As the age of information jets full steam ahead, we are going to see a phenomenal rise in the new entrepreneur and smaller, more specialized enterprises, making today's growth seem minute by comparison.

The question arises: How can a complex, multi-dimensional society function with decision-making vested in thousands of small individual clusters scattered about here and there across the globe? After all, our giant economic, social and political bodies evolved as a means for harmoniously handling large groups of people spread over huge geographical areas. What will be the consequences of entrepreneurship of such sweeping magnitude? Are we destined to become isolated and fragmented, finally falling into entropy for our efforts? I think not. Space and distance per se have little bearing in a high tech society of instantaneous worldwide information dissemination. The maze of impersonal, nonidentifiable and nonaccountable voices of authority emanating from our current systems are long overdue for replacement. The bulk of our present structures have become antiquated and ineffective. This is true at all levels of existence, from an individual, societal, cultural and intercontinental perspective.

Our world tempo is primed for breaking free and going forward to build the solid social fiber that can only stem from shifting responsibility back to each individual. If we look closely we can see these powerful forms taking shape off in the near distance. Here we are about to discover from whence we came and where we are going. Here we will find our meaning and soul. The creation of new paths is ready and waiting. The structure of time is in your hands. And the future destined as you will it.

But are you ready? What about the long investment in your present mode of existence and present career? Is this the hour, the month, the year to make this great decision? Is it time to walk away from your career or have we forgotten something?

When To Walk Away From Your Career

Suppose you have taken a look at your current work situation in view of your new employment standards and it does not measure up. You are ready to quit, take a temporary job for a while and pursue your own thing. In the back of your mind, however, is a bothersome thought. "How", you ask, "can I walk away from a career in which I've put in years of education and training? And what about the long service time on the job? Isn't that admitting to the mistake and waste of all those years?" No. What you did in the past is over and done with. The choices you made were based on your knowledge, information and precepts then. Often we enter into our education and training for an occupation at a very tender age before we have a full vision and enough information from which to choose. Taking responsibility for creating your own world and style of living through your life's mission was probably never seriously considered. Or if it was, you thought of it as something that had to fit together with The Career.

The fact that you are reading this book suggests that whatever your occupational status today, you desire to explore new vistas. Walking away from an occupation is not "throwing it away"; what counts are your choices now. Many persons who have been too busy, caught up in modern living and neglected to reflect on their job situation and how it jells with their personalities, goals and overall satisfaction, are beginning to take stock and seek changes. Generally, some kind of crisis has to occur to prompt action. We see those who are coming up against the mid-life crisis doing complete turnabouts in their professions and personal lives. A plastic surgeon walks away from his wealthy urban patients and opens a bed-and-breakfast inn in a quiet resort town. A divorce attorney finally gets fed up, leaves his practice and moves to a tropical island to teach sailing. A law enforcement officer joins the rodeo.

All of us, for whatever reasons, hate to admit we have made a mistake. This happens in minor as well as major choices. You can probably recall being in an automobile with someone who, on making a wrong turn, continued to go for six or more blocks out of the way in a roundabout fashion rather than admit the mistake, promptly turn back and correct for it. The sooner we are able to consciously assimilate the informational input we have at hand and act on it, the fewer detours we will take through life, and the shorter will be our pathways to prosperity.

In appraising your present occupation, there is a good chance that some of the training and skills you have acquired over the years can be transferred to your new enterprise. It is unlikely that you need to start over from scratch. But if you do, what a wonderful adventure is in store for you!

We tend to postpone making the biggest and toughest decisions in our lives, such as major career and relationship changes. Yet these are the very ones we need to confront and act upon. Having a major unresolved decision facing you is a breeding ground for worry and anxiety.

One reason why we never get around to making the crucial decisions in our lives is that we don't set aside a time out of our daily schedule to physically sit down with a clear head, pen and paper in hand, and draft the pros and cons weighing on our alternatives. Instead, we stuff everything into the far corners of our minds, go on about our affairs, then wonder why petty resentments and angry words burst out of us at the slightest provocation. Worse, in a moment of despair, despondency or depression and with little forethought, we make one of the most important decisions in our lives.

If you are presently working at a job full time and it is in conflict with your entrepreneurial aims, you want to begin exploring new options immediately. *This does not mean quitting.* First, you need to prepare yourself. Before quitting your job and jumping into your own ideas and projects, you want to establish an income stream and become adept at "time structuring"—building time blocks toward your objectives.

We turn now to specific procedures for constructing your days. The first order of business is to minimize any cash flow problems threatening you as a neophyte entrepreneur.

Building Cash Flow Time Blocks

The content of your cash flow time blocks is to focus on the three areas we have just discussed:

(A)Investment procedures;

(B)Changes in your consumers expenditures; and

(C)Temporary employment tactics.

In addition, you are to continue with Time Block 1, your **Millionaire Play Sheet**, and Time Block 3, **Entrepreneur Affirmations**, from the previous chapter. You should be spending approximately thirty minutes each day on these readings and affirmations.

Now, on to Time Blocks 4, 5 and 6.

Time Block No. 4
Investment Procedures

In your weekly calendar, block out one hour, three evenings per week. Fill up this time as follows:

(1)Take three minutes and list all the investment opportunities that you have some familiarity with. For example, these might be stocks, bonds, real estate, CD's, precious metals, money market accounts and mutual funds.

(2)Estimate your personal risk factor. On a scale from 1 to 11 with 11 being high, write down a number which symbolizes the amount of risk you are willing to take. The amount of risk you want to take depends on both your personality and your financial situation. If you tend to be conservative, write down a 1 or 2. While every investment incurs some risk, you minimize this risk by your knowledge and experience.

(3)Take ten minutes to go back over your list and underline those investment opportunities that are the most appealing. What entices you the most?

(4)Next, make a reasonable assessment of the match between your knowledge of the investments you have just underlined and the amount of time it will take before you can begin taking intelligent action. For example, researching and selecting an appropriate mutual fund would be much quicker than becoming involved in something like buying and selling real estate or making decisions on different stocks and bonds.

(5)Based on your analysis, decide on *one type of investment.* Cross out the rest. This might change as your knowledge and situation change, nonetheless, you need to reach a decision point now. This frees up your mind for other activities.

Keep in mind that the most important consideration is the time factor. How much time is it going to take to prepare yourself for making intelligent choices? The hours you want to devote to investments are limited and not your primary interest. Exert caution in selecting an investment that does not require a tremendous amount of time.

To better inform yourself on an investment interest, keep reasonably up-to-date about what is going on in the financial world. This can be done by scanning the front page of the Wall Street Journal, glancing through Barron's, Forbes, Fortune, Money Magazine and listening to weekly television or radio financial reports. Depending on your level of knowledge, taking a look at two or three appropriate books as background for your investment interests is also mandatory. Talking with people in the field can be helpful, however, avoid acting on tips or basing your investment decisions on what everyone else is doing. Often the best strategy is just the opposite! Much good information can be at your fingertips through computer databanks.

Initially, it will take a little time to get your investment decisions squared away. If you only use the three hours a week allotted for this purpose and it takes you two or three weeks total, this is fine. What is important is your consistency in spending time here and that you avoid getting overwhelmed with new information or bogged down in detail.

(6)After you have done your homework, the final step is to actually make the investment. This is the action-step. Once it is accomplished, your investment assignment is complete except for the on-going maintenance of your accounts. Whether you have selected stocks, bonds, a money market account or even a mutual fund, you still want to stay abreast of any news or information that might affect your investments. Continue to spend three hours per week reading and studying the marketplace.

The investment preparation step for entrepreneurship is indispensable to your success and should not be underestimated. It both helps you build the time block habit, and begins to attune your mind toward positive money matters. In the process, you generate more wealth consciousness.

A growing feeling of confidence in the investment arena will free up your mind for entrepreneurial concerns, satisfied that the money you do have currently available is working for you. Later, as your profits grow and you have more capital to invest, you'll have already laid the foundation.

Investment Procedures
Summary of Steps

Step 1: List potential investments.

Step 2: Estimate personal risk factor.
1 2 3 4 5 6 7 8 9 10 11
low high

Step 3: Underline most appealing investments.

Step 4: Assess amount of time to take intelligent action. (in hours)

Step 5: Choose *one investment* and cross out the rest.

Step 6: Follow-through to make investment.

Time Block No. 5
Changes in your Consumer Expenditures

Set aside two hours one evening this week. Use this time to note changes you want to make in your consumer expenditures according to the format below.

(1)On the Play Sheet for Consumer Expenditures on page 114, fill in a dollar amount under "Cost" for your major living expenses: housing, transportation, clothing, insurance, vacation, etc.

(2)Next, consider the Time-Cost Factor for each item. For example, how many months per year are you working on the job to support your automobile costs? How much work time is spent to cover your housing expenses? List estimated time costs for each of your major expenses.

(3)Focus on the alternatives to loosen up more time and money for your entrepreneur projects. Examples would be:

*Cut out the four months per year job time to support your automobile costs and spend this one-third of the year on entrepreneurial pursuits.

*Reduce your housing costs enough to add another month away from your job for entrepreneurial projects.

*Take a vacation closer to home and save travel expenses.

What else can you think of? Don't go overboard in being frugal to the extent that you are worrying about how you spend every nickel. Sometimes it makes sense to splurge and treat yourself. The idea is to have money available for those things you especially want and stop piddling it away on products, services and activities that don't make that much difference to you.

(4)Finally, reach definite decisions on the consumer items you have listed and write down those actions needed to follow through. Block out the earliest time and date for these action steps in your calendar now.

Play Sheet
Consumer Expenditures

	$ Cost	Time-Cost
Housing		
Automobile		
Furniture		
Clothing		
Food		
Entertainment & Recreation		
Vacation		
Gifts		
Other		

Time Block No. 6
Temporary Employment Tactics

After you have a regular routine established for your investment time, and have settled your consumer choices, you are ready to begin temporary employment time tactics. Set aside one hour, three evenings per week for carrying out the procedures contained in this section. Spend this time as follows:

(1)First, list the temporary job possibilities for which you have some training or knowledge. Start with general fields, narrowing the scope as you go along. For example, financial services, the hospitality industry, construction, and computer technology would be a few general fields.

(2)Check them off against your new entrepreneurial criteria: i.e., what requires the least amount of time, energy and pressure?

(3)At this point you may find that you need to gather more information on what opportunities are available in your area. Survey employment agencies, newspaper ads, the yellow pages of your telephone directory and library business directory. Compile specific firms' names, addresses and telephone numbers.

(4)Determine a job search strategy that will take the least amount of time. For instance, group firms in one locale together and make appointments back to back.

(5)Reach a decision point on the most promising temporary employment opportunities. Write these down.

(6)Mark in your calendar specific times and dates when you are going to write, call or personally contact the employers you have selected. Block this time out.

(7)Follow through!

To keep you going on this sometimes tedious and frustrating venture, continually remind yourself of the rewards and riches that are going to be yours by reading over your **Millionaire Play Sheet.**

Temporary Employment Summary of Steps

Step 1: List job possibilities.
Step 2: Check off against new entrepreneurial criteria.
Step 3: Survey temporary job positions.
Step 4: Determine a job search strategy that requires little time.
Step 5: Write down the most promising temporary jobs.
Step 6: Block out time in your calendar to contact each.
Step 7: Follow through.

Solving Cash Flow On-Going Time Blocks

Time Block No. 4 Investment Procedures

Spend three hours per week staying abreast of the marketplace. Make use of select sources such as computer databanks, newsletters, hot lines, cable television, special reports and other media which may have a bearing on your investments. Include both general, background information sources as well as more specific data. Use this time also to make any changes in your investment portfolio.

Time Block No. 5 Changes in your Consumer Expenditures

Spend a minimum of one-half hour per week taking the action steps necessary for changes in your consumer expenditures.

Time Block No. 6 Temporary Employment Tactics

Spend at least five hours per week following through on your job search until appropriate temporary employment is secured.

Block these times out in your calendar now!

4
Nonstructured Time & The Creative Enterprise

"If I bind the future I bind my will. If I bind my will I strangle creation."

—GEORGE BERNARD SHAW

The Stress of Nonstructured Time

As you get further removed from the boundaries of a clearly defined occupational structure, you are left wide open to a host of new questions and choices. Gone is the safe 9-to-5 routine, leaving you with both the challenge and discomfort of myriad decision points. And the stress of these unfamiliar decision grounds can quickly become overwhelming. According to one astute social scientist, Julian Jaynes, the state of uncertainty attached to decision-making is precisely what stress is all about. Few of us have developed the personal resources to competently cope with this phenomenon. It is one of the reasons we so often see someone who has retired from long years of work rushing back into the job market shortly thereafter. Regardless of how bad a job might be, there is the comfortable security of having your hours cut out for you. Each day is ordered around specific time frames.

Now, out on your own, the sun comes up and goes down at the same time, but the minutes and hours in between hang there, almost maliciously, daring you to venture forth and make your mark in the world or fall from their weight. Suddenly, the burden of responsibility looms before you. You feel at once the excitement of possibility in the air, at the same time an urge to grab hold of something familiar and be freed from the burden of consequential decision-making.

In the country of Sweden where the individual is allowed more personal freedom and choice than any other nation, we find one of the world's highest suicide rates. And in most of our Western nations where there is a great amount of leisure and potential opportunity, a high percentage of us turn to excessive alcohol, drugs and other time escape mechanisms. As you embark on your own, how can you guard against the perils of undue stress stemming from lack of structure and choice overload?

It has been said that "You cannot discover new oceans unless you have the courage to lose sight of the shore". Nonetheless, leaving behind what is known and familiar to investigate new worlds can be hazardous to your physical and mental health if you have not acquired good navigational tools. As the old occupational structures collapse behind you along with your former identity, you need to have a spirit empowered with the ability to create anew at every turn, and be able to steer on course even in the face of turbulent waters. For out of each choice, the foundation for your future success is laid.

The majority of us postpone making decisions as long as we can. We have a habit of looking to others for guidance, approval and assurance that we are doing the right thing. We'd rather do just about anything than take on the responsibility for making tough choices with big consequences. Out on your own, this kind of stance won't get you even a fraction of the way to financial success. The entrepreneurial path is strewn with choices, some minor but others with far-reaching effects. Ducking responsibility here is a sure-fire route to frustration and failure.

The transition stage between being an employee and being an entrepreneur is crucial to your future success. You stand at the crossroads of creating a new personal world of prosperity and riches, and in the process a slice of the larger universe. As you leave the old structures behind, however, and before the new patterns become established, you are prone to slide into a random activity routine at the mercy of whatever happens to come up, subject to the pressures of the moment. A typical day might look like that of my friend, Roberta, an intelligent woman in her mid-thirties who recently quit work as a stock broker to pursue an interest in music therapy and consulting. A Wednesday taken from her daily log is given on the next page.

Roberta's Daily Log

7:00 a.m.	Awake, lie in bed thinking about what to do first, daydream about different possibilities for getting the business started.
8:00 a.m.	Up, shower, breakfast and conversation with sweetheart.
9:00 a.m.	Make bed, read newspaper, catch program on television.
10:00 a.m.	Go into town, check out offices to rent.
11:00 a.m.	Back at home, make a few phone calls, set up appointments at two banks to discuss the business and raise some capital.
12:00 noon	Lunch with a friend.
1:00 p.m.	Sit down to do some projections on a consulting project.
2:00 p.m.	Interrupted by phone calls from acquaintances.
3:00 p.m.	Have a snack and settle back into the project.
4:00 p.m.	Kids come home from school and talk about their day.
5:30 p.m.	Watch the news on television.
6:00 p.m.	Dinner.
7:30 p.m.	Prepare notes for club meeting.
8:45 p.m.	Attend professional women's club meeting, preside as acting vice-president.
11:00 p.m.	Go to bed.

The biggest mistake is not so much in the content of what Roberta is doing, but in the lack of choice, the drifting into whatever happens to come up, with little conscious choice and awareness of the disempowering consequences of succumbing to an unproductive daily routine.

During this critical period of your entrepreneurship, you need to be fully cognizant of the dynamics of each day and its impact on your success. Sliding into a comfortable routine of activities, whether productive or nonproductive, will save you from the stress of daily choices. This is why so many of us are easy targets for all the circumstantial stimuli that befall us. To escape from these disempowering influences you need to divide your hours up consciously, in a fashion where time spent in each area of your life is a true representation of what you actually want it to be.

As an entrepreneur, you are subject to a constant change of events. And each time you break from one routine into another, you are bumped back into the jaws of nonstructured time. This is not something to avoid. It is something to acknowledge, understand and eventually delight in as your confidence and creative powers grow.

Your first hurdle is to start setting up your new living arrangement in a manner which provides for all the vital areas of your life. This helps prevent conflicts from erupting later on. Included in your list would be the consideration of time allotment for health and fitness maintenance, personal relationships, family and friends and educational growth. Ask yourself, "What is the smartest allotment of time in each area of my life so that I stay pivoted toward opportunity, profit and peace of mind?"

The steps at the end of this chapter help you lay out a comprehensive time frame for each of the principal dimensions of your life. You may be of a mind to pretend that some basic needs do not exist in your passion to get started with a project. This is both good and bad. It is good if you have thought through your priorities and know where you stand. You always want to keep moving forward with a single minded purpose. If you neglect coming to grips with all the dimensions of your life, however, problems will inevitable surface at the most inopportune times.

I repeatedly see instances of this among my colleagues and clients. Marvin had been in business for himself nineteen months and was on the verge of closing a long-sought contract that could be worth hundreds of thousands of dollars to his firm. To secure the contract he needed to take an unexpected plane trip immediately to Tokyo. Pulling at his heartstrings, however, was his only daughter's high school graduation ceremony. There was no way that he could attend the ceremony and be in Tokyo for the meeting. Misgivings and guilt plagued him as he got on the plane for Tokyo.

Loraine, a retired paralegal secretary, decided to do her own thing late in life. At age fifty-two she began putting in twelve hour days in the mail order business, unwittingly neglecting time with her mate. She soon noticed that he was becoming despondent and drinking too much. Although she wanted to meet more of his expectations, with the demands of building up a flourishing enterprise, it had proved impossible. Now just as she was at a critical stage in her marketing program, Loraine discovered that her husband's drinking was completely out of control. Decisions needed to be made on the home front. Guilt was interfering with business and she wondered whether she was about to lose both a husband and her business.

Situations such as these are commonplace, and are a major factor in business failure and personal stress. To reach the fine heights of success, you cannot let yourself constantly be torn this way and that. Therefore, at the onset of your entrepreneurial pursuits you need to lay out a viable time allocation program which is comprehensive enough to cover all the areas of your life, including how you intend to deal with the unexpected.

Although you can never know exactly what sort of problems, conflicts and obstacles might get strewn in your path, you can equip your mind and emotions to deal effectively and nonstressfully with whatever comes up. This is accomplished through sensitive time structuring and has nothing to do with making lists of potential problems and solutions. More will be said about this shortly. *The grande resource you are targeting is your creative mind state within the context of time.*

Remember the saying, "A river doesn't stop for obstacles or things that get in the way. It keeps on going wherever it is going because it is a river and that's what rivers do." Settle in your heart and mind the value of your entrepreneurial commitment now and recognize that you need to be doing exactly what you consciously choose for yourself. You are to answer to no one but yourself. Indeed, you will find that you are your toughest critic. Once you are clear about where you stand in relation to all the dimensions of your life, your choices will follow almost automatically, without self-reprisal, anxiety, guilt or any other damaging emotional baggage.

Mostly, it is the little things that keep us from giving full service to our mission in life. Setting up a living arrangement to allow for each fundamental aspect of your life (health and fitness, family, friends and spiritual needs) will act as a safeguard against hidden time wasters in your day. Some of the most menacing time wasters are all about us. Sitting around watching TV soaps, drinking coffee, reading the newspaper, smoking cigarettes, talking idly on the telephone, munching snacks, making excessive shopping or grocery trips and other purposeless activities quickly swallow up the minutes and hours.

Top self-made entrepreneurs unfailingly place a high premium on the minutes of each day. The unsuccessful, on the other hand, are notorious for their flagrant misuse and disregard for time. Ed Beckly, the young and successful real estate tycoon has offered this sage piece of advice: "If you really want to be rich, watch what the poor do and then don't do it."

As an entrepreneur, no one is standing over you telling you what to do or directing your time. This is an art you must start mastering at once. Until you have learned how to reorient yourself in the entrepreneurial time frame, your days are going to be bridled with stress and lackluster living. Indeed, *total personal time management is the ultimate encounter with stress.* Until you learn how to line up the hours in your day appropriate to your goals, you are wide open to the vulnerability of every instant and the nuisance of every distraction.

When we walk into our homes at night we can easily flick a switch and have the light come on automatically and predictably. Pushing our own buttons to get a desired effect turns out to be much more complex. A familiar triangle is: (A)You have a need or want. (B)You set a goal. (C)You obtain the necessary information to get you from A to B. So far so good. But what happens? How often we set out to do something then find that our behavior is totally out of whack with what we intended and wanted. You want to eat less and stop smoking so you'll have more energy for your entrepreneurial objectives. You want to establish a better relationship with your mate so there will be no more energy-draining hassles. You would dearly love to get the formal business plan brewing in your head down on paper so you can obtain a loan. And poof, like lightning, the minutes, hours, weeks fly by and you are no further along than you were months or even years ago in achieving your objectives. We find ourselves locked into unproductive, unsatisfying time habit patterns. As Emerson in his ***Power*** essay has observed, "No matter how much faculty of idle seeing a (person) has, the step from knowing to doing is rarely taken".

Intending to do something, then being unable to follow through results in lowered self-esteem and an emotional state that ranges from mild irritation and frustration to troubling attacks of anxiety and depression, a state clearly anathema to the arrival of riches in your life. The greater the gap between what you think you should be doing and what you are actually doing, the more stress you feel. So far as we know, homo sapiens is the only conscious entity in existence who has the power to set personal goals, plan a course of action, then take the necessary steps to follow thorough. What goes wrong that we so frequently flub up? Why does getting from "A" to "B" pose such a dilemma for the vast majority of us?

As a nation we have learned how to reach new planets, orbit the moon and build giant technological and financial networks, yet the seemingly simple task of rationally directing our own behavior and time in our best interests eludes us or at best, proceeds at a snail's pace. Herein lies humanity's more pressing and dramatic task. And for the first period in history, as we move from a society of employees to a society of entrepreneurs, we have the discretionary time, fresh burst of awareness and inchoate urgency to solve this great problem.

Making your own personal breakthrough in closing the gap between the actual and the ideal, between what you are doing and what you desire to be doing, will result in a thrill of victory exceeding the most momentous occasion. To shape and mold your time and behavior in a manner that expresses your uniqueness, where there is minimal conflict of values, goals and action patterns, and concurrently create a prosperity outcome to leave your special imprint on the world of today and tomorrow is truly what life is all about.

Today's entrepreneur is a precursor of tomorrow's future, a world that will likely be totally dissimilar to our present occupationally structured society. The new age being ushered in is sprouting a breed of entrepreneurs with a vision and personality quite different from the old cast. In the past, many of those who struggled on their own had no choice, nor did they have the thousands of occupations from which to choose. Now the prospective entrepreneur is looking at the options open to him within the present system and rejecting them, making a conscious choice to build a reality more in keeping with his vision of what can be. This is rarely an easy choice. With the multitude of work-for-wages jobs available, the seemingly easier route is to get a job and let an employer plan your time and pay you a salary. You walk into a ready-made structure, know pretty much what you're getting, and let the employer bear the brunt of the responsibility for whatever happens. It takes courage and a very special personality to forge ahead on your own in our present day and age. Yet this is exactly what we see happening.

And the giant corporations, IBM, General Motors, Exxon, Mobil, sense the threat to themselves and are making every attempt to lure these bright entrepreneurial spirits back into their tracks. Hold firm! You will be rewarded.

Successful entrepreneurship in contemporary society requires different motivational and cognitive skills than those usually found within the large corporate work setting. Unless you take over an existing business or model your new enterprise closely after another, you will be required to make more extensive use of what have been referred to as right brain functions: spatial thinking, creative processes and holistic organizational modes. The surge of literature on right brain—left brain styles over the past decade is certainly timely for the expansion of today's entrepreneurial world.

How do you get started then in carving out this new prosperity? How do you handle being thrown back on yourself after all the years of others by and large managing your time: first your parents at home, then your teachers in the classroom and finally your bosses in the workplace? What steps need to be taken to set up your days, weeks and months precisely right for your personality to insure the basic requisites of good living: optimal physical and mental health, enjoyable sexual relations, supportive friends, plus all the other benefits? When your day is no longer ordered around the job, how shall the time chunks most potently be divided between rest, sleep, social contacts, recreation, maintenance needs and play projects to accelerate your personal and financial fantasies?

This quandary should not be taken lightly. While about anyone you ask will self-righteously proclaim, "I certainly know what to do with my time. I just don't have enough of it!" On the contrary, I have found very, very few people have much regard for or make good use of the bulk of their discretionary time. All you need do to be convinced is look around you. Check out people waiting for planes at the airport or wandering through a shopping center and grocery store. Look in on any doctor's or dentist's office and other establishments. People everywhere are killing time. We sit idly in restaurants and cocktail lounges eating and drinking too much. And at home we mesmerize ourselves in front of the video screen and behind the daily newspaper. Setting aside time for relaxation and recreational needs can be beneficial, but falling out of pace with our purpose via the unplanned daily tide of circumstantial events seriously undermines the fiber of our being, and leads straight down the road to failure.

There seems to be a direct correlation between the amount of free time we have available and our misuse. Just as rare commodities, diamonds and rubies, are more highly valued and prized, so it is with our time. When we don't have any, as when someone else is controlling us and has ownership over our time (for example, in a possessive relationship, in a rigid work setting or in prison), we would practically sell our soul to regain some of our lost freedom. Then, as soon as we are handed a large amount, say in retirement, an extended vacation, or in the breakup of a bad personal relationship, we go crazy, piddling away masses of minutes, taking twice as long to do the most mundane chores, dabbling at this and that, and skipping from one activity to another with little sense of comprehension about what's going on and the wasted potential in our life. All about us, we see people squandering time as casually as the ocean waves wash away sand castles along the beach.

What is the solution? Is there some kind of unifying principle to tie together all the bits and pieces of our lives so that we can proceed consistently on target toward riches and well-being? Yes, there is. In the preceding chapters you took the first steps toward structuring your free time and learning to build time blocks in keeping with your objectives. Now I want to introduce you to the creative process of time and show you how it impacts on entrepreneurship and riches.

As a starting point, begin approaching your nonwork hours with the same kind of problem-solving abilities that are used to achieve business success in the occupational setting. That is, you need to have a clear sense of purpose, determine your primary interests, set goals, lay out a plan of action and develop strategies to bring about the desired results. As you re-establish your priorities and target completion dates, you are to structure your time accordingly.

The difficulty that most of us get into once we leave the employee routine behind is that we are unsure about which direction to take. "What", you wonder, "is the best route to financial independence and wealth?" If you are like most people, you have many interests and ideas that could result in riches. What selection method do you use to sift through all the possibilities? Also, over the years your major interests, goals and objectives change. How can you protect yourself against making choices that lock you into an enterprise which you may later come to regret?

There are no easy answers to these questions, and your search is to be a lifelong quest. The assignment for the moment, however, to initiate motion along the right course, is to simply reflect on what you truly enjoy most. What gives you the greatest amount of satisfaction? In the next chapter you will be shown a seven step procedure for identifying those projects best suited to your special personality. Here we are laying the foundation for your journey and vision. It is through the creative process of time that you discover how to orient your life's enterprise. Let's take a closer look at this intriguing phenomenon and how it relates to your problem-solving capabilities, playful nature and wealth.

Problem-Solving, Creativity & Play

One of the best known popular books on our problem-solving nature and how this faculty of mind relates to financial gain is *Think and Grow Rich* by Napoleon Hill. Hill's book is packed with truth and inspirational messages especially applicable to those individuals who made up America's pioneer years as a struggling industrial nation. Today as we have grown into a vast, informational network stretching across the oceans through outer space, our quest continues for a better way of life. It is in part due to the scientific and technological developments evolving from our basic problem-solving nature that we have the leisure or free time to turn our attention at this point in history to the most promising challenge of all: recognizing why we are here, confronting it, and living it—taking full responsibility for creating our own personal world by shaping time in a way that is consistent with our purpose and being. At last, we can explore the vital questions of life, not like an elite class of philosophers of old did, but from the firm foundation of our present individual scientific stance.

With our newfound freedom and knowledge we are poised to break out of the metaphysical circle of speculations that led nowhere and arrive at rare horizons of self-world understanding and personal riches. Today, as we release ourselves from the occupational prison that has bound and decentered us, we have the chance to recapture and restructure the time commodity in tune with our special uniqueness, emphasizing and expanding on the ways in which we are different, rather than trying to adapt and plug ourselves into slots that we're not. Here is where the work ethic with its nose-to-the-grindstone, slave-away-for-a-rainy-day mentality, falls apart.

For man and woman are more than mere thinking, problem-solving entities; we are a race of playful, emotional and curious creatures with an unquenching thirst and passion for understanding and vital self-expression. We have learned much about the "how" of our surroundings, how to take things apart and put them back together. We know how to build cars, skyscrapers, televisions and jets. We can make mechanical hearts, computer microchips and simulated diamonds and pearls. But the "why" of it all has remained shrouded in mystery. Attempts to put the segments of our lives together into an integrated whole and orchestrate each to the tune of an overall purpose and plan have by and large met with frustration and confusion. Ever since the Golden Age of Greek Civilization with its powerful insights pushed the great questions to the limit, we have backed off, leaving the riddles unanswered as we go about our business designing and building the technological marvels we take so much for granted.

Only recently have we attempted to come back to the mother of all our motivations and desires, the quest to understand, and live life fully within that understanding. Our lapse of memory has been only temporary, the intent has always been there, waiting for a moment in history when the odds for success would be more favorable. As the year 2000 approaches, our scientific know-how coupled with discretionary time stands before us, permitting each person to put his or her life on a plane of cohesive understanding rather than be subject to the piecemeal state of existence we have known. Now the strands of our being can be intertwined in harmony, leaving us free from the disjointed lifestyle that has torn us to and fro. As we travel forward in our greater perspective we will be putting to rest the raging wars of man-against-man, man-against-self and man-against-nature. Conflicts and strife will become a thing of the past, of an antiquated age, replaced by a dynamic concordant effect blossoming forth from the individual center outward into new forms of reality.

In the century we leave behind, we have attempted to align ourselves with work settings that were somewhat compatible with our personality and seek outlets there for self-expression, creativity and financial gain. Though never a realistic stance, the occupational era has been a necessary chain in the events leading to the evolution of our current personal freedom and individual nucleus of power. As an increasing number of our present corporations and institutions have become skewed in their dysfunctional aspects, the viable course of action calls for channeling our creative endeavors outside of the existing systems and into the development of alternative forms as entrepreneurs.

An extraordinary opportunity awaits each of us today to break the stronghold of those trends precipitating the demise of humankind, and in the process, plump up our own individual riches. Furthermore, you needn't feel uneasy about the pairing of the one relatively lofty societal goal with a more self-serving objective since the two are as compatible as sunshine and blue skies. When you strike the right chord in your own existence through creative ventures, a positive reverberation is felt within the culture and world of which you are a part. The two go hand in hand. On the opposite tack, when you act in ways that are detrimental to yourself, you are quite probably hurting others as well. When each of us follows our own creative bent, a better world unfolds for everyone.

Let's dwell more completely into this phase of our existence. What exactly does creativity entail and how is it related to your financial independence? It is through the creative act that you express your uniqueness as an individual to leave your special imprint on the universe, and in this action, affirm your self-worth and attract riches. It is also in this process that you discover your mission and direction in life. On the downside, when this creativity is prevented from evolving, you feel as if you are nothing, empty and without meaning. In order to escape from this void, busyness usually sets in. You scurry about doing a little of this and a little of that, soon having a plethora of activities depleting your time. While many of the ways in which you spend your time could be called worthwhile, the "loose ends" of your existence continually crop up to get in the way. Whenever you get too far off course and removed from your intended purpose, you feel you are "not yourself" and "not right somehow". That's because you aren't. You cannot expect to deny the lifeblood and soul of you and have any peace with yourself. The deepest sense of satisfaction and joy in living comes when you are true to your creative nature. What I'd like you to aim for is a broader viewpoint and action synergism so that each facet of your life takes shape with respect to your central creative thrust.

But what is this nebulous thing we are labeling "creativity"? Surveying the literature, we find creativity delineated as a smorgasbord of sentiments, emotions and behaviors. Both social scientists and popular writers have had difficulty pinning down this dynamic concept. Creativity has variously been viewed as (A)a *process* (the ways in which we think, feel and play around with ideas and symbols in our heads); (B)a *product* (an external behavior, service or tangible item); and (C)a *potential* (a capacity or talent which has not yet become evident). Let's break these down and look at each in the light of entrepreneurship.

Creativity as process

One component of creativity as process is the number of ideas you can come up with when presented with a problem. Problems might be specific or general. For instance, you might be asked to brainstorm about all the different uses a chair could be put to. It could be used to stand on, to lean against, to rock in and to sleep on. With a little thought you could probably come up with a dozen other uses, some of which might lead to new furniture designs. A more general and complex problem posed is "What can be done to relieve stress?" Ideas you might list are "to mediate, have a physical workout, laugh a lot, listen to the ocean waves and go on vacation". These in turn may prompt additional remedies.

Another aspect of the process component of creativity is how your ideas differ from someone else's. How many of the ideas that pop out of your head are original and unduplicated by the majority of other people pondering the same problem? Some people are good at coming up with many ideas when presented with a task while others tend to be less fluent, however, the ideas which they do have are more original.

The best ideas for entrepreneurial projects frequently originate from personal experience as we go about our day-to-day affairs. Margo, an acquaintance of mine living in San Francisco, recently spoke to me about her friend, Ted, who resides in Chicago. His birthday was coming up and she wanted to send him something special but had limited time to shop around, wrap and mail a gift. She also had a tight budget. Considering what to do, she thought about hiring a shopping service but the cost was more than she wanted to spend. Calling up a relative in Ted's area and asking her to pick out a present was another option. Sending money in a card was another not very imaginative possibility. A local florist could be contacted and a nice plant wired, but Ted wasn't that interested in greenery. Margo had come up with four ideas, none of which adequately solved the problem. If she didn't care much about her friend and had no emotional involvement in the decision, it wouldn't matter. She probably would have acted on the first option that came to mind and given it no further thought. In that case, there wouldn't really be a problem, and there would be no room for creativity.

Her objective though was to do something special for her friend. "Wouldn't it be great", she thought, "If there was a national wire service similar to the floral wire service, but that had a variety of gift items, perhaps colorful baskets of fruits and cheeses, a basket arrangement of wine and glasses, or maybe some fun gadgetry items where all I had to do was pick up the phone, use my credit card, give them my friend's address and have everything taken care of?"

What you want to get in the habit of doing in common situations like this is opening your mind to new possibilities, and generating solutions that have not yet been done (so far as you know). Ideas are precipitated in part due to an emotional involvement and concern about the issue at hand, along with your degree of interest. Out of this kind of creative process, entrepreneurship is born: keeping your eyes peeled for different needs as you go about your daily activities. Whenever you are frustrated over being unable to find an existing service or product to meet your needs, there is a good chance others are seeking the same thing or something similar.

Creativity as product

Generating ideas and coming up with original solutions will not make you money unless you act on them. In the example just cited, someone did just this. Gift wire services now flourish in cities across the United States. This is where creativity as *product* comes in. An idea is crystalized, then implemented in the marketplace. The gem of an idea need not both originate and be implemented by the same person. An enterprising person can purchase someone else's idea or take an existing product and discover a different, more profitable way of marketing it. This is the action step of creativity. As your creativity is tapped within the entrepreneurial domain, you will discover your own inclinations and where your time is most profitably spent.

Creativity as potential

Finally, when we speak of someone's *creative potential,* the third component, we could be referring to a child's future behavior or anyone who has not as yet made the choice to follow through on their latent creative capacity. Virtually everyone has creative potential. It is a matter of degree and whether or not it has been put into practice. Generally speaking, creativity is best thought of as some combination of process, product and potential.

Threads of creativity: timelessness & playfulness

Since creativity has so frequently been confused with thinking and problem-solving, it is well to ask, "How does creativity differ from intelligence and problem-solving?" This issue has been a source of controversy among investigators for many years. Some social scientists have even questioned whether it makes any sense to talk about creativity as a separate psychological dimension. Current research and empirical data suggest that there is little justification for making any distinction between creativity and problem-solving unless we take into account the elements of freedom and playfulness. The distinguishing qualities that highly creative persons have in common are a concern with associative freedom and a playful, permissive task attitude. That is to say, the conditions under which you perform need to be free of time constraints imposed by others. And in order to give full expression to your creative talents, an attitude of playfulness and total absorption in the task before you is required. Einstein, for example, has talked about the need for "associative play" and "combinatory play" in ideas and images. It is this playing around with ideas, symbols and images that sparks inventions.

Creativity, let me underscore, is not something reserved for brilliant minds, nor does it presuppose making major contributions in the arts, humanities or sciences. Within each person's individuality lies a creative domain. This is what makes you different and special. And it is from this domain that your conscious being evolves. Your particular creative inclinations could lie in home decorating, innovative cooking methods, rebuilding old cars, marketing techniques or a thousand other activities. The magnitude of your contribution is immaterial. What is important is that you tap your creativity to its greatest potential, both for the self-enrichment and mind-expansion rewards it affords as well as financial remunerations. Sustenance of a wealth consciousness within the realm of your activities is cardinal. Without this, an imbalance is likely to result, producing conflicts of interest on how your time should be divided. If you are caught up in creative endeavors that have no chance of bringing in dollars and you must forever scramble around searching for jobs to put food on the table and pay the bills, you are going to be a bundle of nerves. This lack of resolution between primary interests (what you truly *want* to do) and earning money (what you feel you *have* to do) is a breeding ground for insecurity and impoverishment.

Essential for creative expression is freedom from externally imposed time constraints, and the approaching of your tasks and goals with a playful spirit. You will find that your creativity flourishes most when you are void of pressures, demands and obligations. This doesn't mean that you should have no regard for time or its boundaries. Nor does it mean that you want to be negligent in keeping your appointments and responsibilities to others. It is your internal mind state that is crucial. For example, suppose you have scheduled the hours between six and nine p.m. to attend to one of your entrepreneurial projects. During that period you need to let yourself completely go to become immersed in the task at hand, with a mind uncluttered by future "must do's", "should do's", or any thoughts of deadlines and failure.

It is in this state of complete absorption and freedom that you are able to experience the joy of timelessness reported by Eastern philosophers, and out of which your consciousness is extended to reap new creations. Your attention is focused fully in the present moment, free of any past failures or the possibility of future mishaps. At this juncture, you neither evaluate, judge nor worry about your activities, but frolic in the delight of new forms and combinations and the surprise of outcome.

One of the biggest deterrents to entrepreneurial success is an attitude beset by worries over past mistakes, "can't do's" and fear of failures. We can learn much from Thomas Edison's creative attitude. When asked how he could continue working in view of his hundreds of failures, he replied, "I have not failed once." For him, every outcome was of interest and a worthwhile endeavor, irrespective of whether it was in keeping with his predictions. "Failure" did not exist within his frame of reference. Nor should it in yours. Every act of purpose, made in good faith and good conscience has meaning regardless of how trivial it seems at the time. Indeed, many of our greatest inventions have come about through serendipity. More will be said about this interesting phenomenon and its bearing on your success in a later chapter.

Characteristics of Creative Persons & Entrepreneurs

Emanating from the spirit of playfulness are a number of attributes and personality characteristics found in success-bound creative persons. They tend to be fiercely independent, having a mind of their own that is uneasily influenced by others. Their energy is intensely channeled in one direction at a time. Many creative persons are likely to be referred to by associates as loners, be sometimes misunderstood and have a low interest in social activities. Their preferences are frequently for mental manipulations involving ideas and symbols rather than people. Most of all, they have a strong desire to pit themselves against uncertain circumstances in which their own effort is the deciding factor.

Each of these qualities has a bearing on your success as an entrepreneur. It is imperative that you have the self-direction, single-minded purpose, perseverance and freedom from distraction to follow through on your projects. Also essential is that you act confidently even in the face of an uncertain outcome.

Creativity as used here assumes a socially useful and desirable product, service or event. It is in the discovery of how you can best express your uniqueness—the creative crystal that only you can contribute to society, the soul of you that validates your existence and reason for being, and from which you evolve to an even higher plane of awareness—that you will know entrepreneurial success and the riches of the universe.

Michael Phillips, the inventor of Master Charge has said: "The hardest thing to convince people is a fact that only the very rich know: The way to make a lot of money is to do exactly what you want to do and do it exactly the way you want to do it". You will reach the pinnacle of success when you discover what your unique blend of personality lends itself to, *what you truly want to do,* and have the courage to act on it.

Observe the similarity between qualities of creative persons and characteristics of the entrepreneur. The entrepreneur is by and large a highly creative person. More importantly, this creativity does not stop at the idea level or at the hobby level but is manifest in an incessant profit-mindedness. The true entrepreneur has a penchant for seeing opportunities all about him or her.

Studies on entrepreneurs have flourished recently. Most of these have dealt with easily identifiable demographical and sociological variables such as one's order of birth, ethnic origin and age. Among these studies there is a general consensus on a number of findings. Entrepreneurs tend to be getting younger and we see many at their peak before they reach forty-five. They are ethnically diverse and number high in the minority groups. Often they have dropped out of college and are more likely to be "C" students or have inconsistent grades, for example, "A's" as well as "D's", apparently pursuing those courses which they especially enjoy and have a knack for to the neglect of others. Entrepreneurs frequently have a dislike for team sports, are less likely to be joiners and show little interest in country club socializing. A larger percentage have been born in poverty or experienced hardships in growing up. At this writing the rate of women entrepreneurs is increasing at five times the rate for men according to a report in the Wall Street Journal.

Irrespective of the foregoing, you should be cautioned in surmising that there is any one type of entrepreneur. This is misleading. There is no one kind of entrepreneur. And it is simplistic to say that there is a main type of entrepreneurial personality. While there are some common denominators, they come in a variety of packages. Looking into the future, I believe we will find that most of the demographical factors itemized above on which entrepreneurs are found to differ from the general population will diminish in importance. People from all walks of life are joining the ranks of entrepreneurs.

On the other hand, the attitudinal and motivational characteristics of entrepreneurs that I have been describing will be more dominant and evident in the future. It matters little whether you are female or first born. And it is of no consequence whether you are gentile or Jewish, have a Ph.D. or have dropped out of college. What makes the difference is that you learn and then apply the fine art of entrepreneurship. To advance you further in this direction, let's take a closer look at those qualities and distinctions found in the entrepreneur's lifestyle and which were touched on briefly in an earlier chapter.

Productive time habits

At the center of the successful entrepreneur's lifestyle is the ability to take charge of his or her time. Entrepreneurs value time. And it is from this nucleus that prosperity springs. They delight in scheduling their own time blocks and working on their own, finding it easy to allocate the minutes and hours in accord with priorities. High success entrepreneurs seem almost to have a sixth sense about how to maneuver the operatives in their environment so that everything falls profitably into place. This is what you are to learn and put into practice.

While most of us are vulnerable to time wasters, top entrepreneurs have virtually eliminated the three major classes of time and energy abusers. These include (1)External sources of time wasters; (2)Internal mechanisms and (3)Excessive habit patterns that act to squander time. To help you ward off these success robbers, some definitions are in order.

External time wasters

External sources are all those phenomena outside of you that intrude on your time. Examples are: unplanned telephone calls, unexpected visitors, distracting noise, demands by others and commuting time. Successful entrepreneurs have discovered how to arrange their physical space, their time and work environment, in a way that minimizes such interferences. For instance, to reduce commuting time, they are likely to set up shop close to home or at home. And to handle their business affairs more efficiently, they look for a work site that is free from distracting noises, social interferences and temptations.

Internal time wasters

Internal time wasters are the mental and emotional activities that go on inside your head. These are the most deadly to your success. They include procrastination, unresolved conflicts, frustration, anxiety and worry. Mark Twain once said, "I'm an old man and I've had many troubles, most of which have never happened." Worry, anxiety, resentments and anger are your worst time killers. True entrepreneurs have learned how to keep them out of their day.

Excessive habit patterns

Finally, the third category of time abusers is the excesses in your life, especially as they apply to your health habits. These include overeating, drinking and smoking too much and any other excessive behavior patterns that act to slow you down and squelch your time. Successful entrepreneurs have established sound diet and exercise habits to maximize their energy level, stay alert and have razor sharp judgment in their business dealings. Too many of us believe that the only way to stay healthy is to eat what we don't want, drink what we don't like, and do what we'd rather not. In reality, establishing habits that promote your physical well-being (and riches) are simply a matter of using the appropriate strategies and techniques to structure your time and space.

Once established, good habits are just as difficult to break as bad habits. I'm sure you can point to some exceptions: a person you know who has violated every good health rule and still makes top dollar. This is possible, but why? Your aim is to have everything working in your favor. Why put a yoke around your neck when you don't have to? It's far easier to establish good physical fitness habits. By the time you finish reading this book you are not only going to *want* to bring about these positive changes in your life, but will be well on the way to *being* a model entrepreneur and *enjoying* every step of the way.

Unproductive time habits are best eliminated by focusing on your objectives: knowing exactly what you want, and planning your days accordingly. Your aim is to crystallize your goals and values in terms of time commitments. Otherwise you'll find yourself forever getting side-tracked, off course and taking so many detours that you are old and weary before you have discovered the financial independence and riches available to you.

Though it sometimes seems that we have all the time in the world, this is not the case. Each minute and each day is more important than you can ever imagine. And the closer you come to taking charge of your time, arranging your hours in a way that aligns with your personality and goals, the more wonderful surprises life holds in store for you.

An action-orientation

Entrepreneurs' sense of the time value is reflected in their modes of planning and action styles. They move with a feeling of urgency and purpose, as if they have a mission in life, which indeed we all do. They have set long term goals as well as short term objectives. Their goal-setting, however, incorporates a more unified, action-oriented approach than is usually found in the traditional types of goal setting where everything is laid out in advance. One researcher, David McClelland, founder of the Boston based foundation, McBer and Company, has referred to this as "goalless planning". In other words, the entrepreneur will often set out on a mission without knowing exactly how he or she is going to get there. They do not wait until all the information is in, or until everything is all figured out before getting their feet wet, but act... and then correct as more is learned about the situation and as feedback becomes available.

An almost feverish desire to get started is exhibited. Successful entrepreneurs are first and foremost do-ers over thinkers, and have a restless need for getting things done. As a result, they may be short tempered with those around them who act to slow down the process. They adhere to the motto, "With all thy getting, get going" and prefer to work with others who have a similar action-orientation. Entrepreneurs know that "All things come to him or her who goes after them."

Decisiveness

Consistent with this action-orientation is the entrepreneur's decisiveness. They are impatient with the sluggish decision-making process often found in large corporations and tend to avoid meetings and other situations that waste time.

Highly success-minded, they have the courage to act in the face of uncertainty and are not overly concerned about making mistakes. Entrepreneurs realize that "genius makes the most mistakes" and if their batting average is only fifty-one per cent they come out ahead. While they have a knack for picking people's brains and learning from others' successes and failures, when required, they have no hesitation about trying new approaches and learn quickly from their own experiences. As Peter Drucker, the well-known management expert, has so aptly stated: "The future will not just happen if one wishes hard enough. It requires decision—*now*. It imposes risk—*now*. It requires action—*now*."

Risk-taking power

Entrepreneurs are often viewed as gamblers and high rollers. In truth, this is a somewhat exaggerated characteristic. The successful person has the courage to act in the face of unknown outcomes, but is more likely to take well-calculated risks over big gambles. A recent Gallup Poll published in the Wall Street Journal on entrepreneurs showed many of them to display a cautious, even prudent side in their business dealings. Also, while entrepreneurs thrive on seeking out challenges and becoming involved in what others may perceive as high-risk ventures, in *their eyes,* based on the ultra-confidence in their own abilities to pull it off, the risk is not so great as viewed from another's standpoint. Richard Clements, the highly ambitious and creative architect, told me during a personal interview, "Other people think I take tremendous risks, but I know I'm a very capable person so while what I do seems risky to others, it doesn't seem so risky to me."

A strong belief in themselves

Entrepreneurs have a strong belief in themselves and delight in pitting themselves against seemingly insurmountable odds. There is a charisma and power about them, a mastery over time and circumstances that is able to overcome all obstacles. Indeed, they know no obstacles. "Obstacles", they are quick to tell you, "are what you see when you take your eyes off the goal". They are confident in their ability to find a way over, around or under whatever gets in the way. Like Thomas Edison with his one hundred attempts to invent the lightbulb, failure is not a word in their vocabulary.

Tenacity

While most of us still adhere to the motto: "If at first you don't succeed, forget it", entrepreneurs consistently act as if a successful outcome is imminent. They refuse to take "no" for an answer and persevere until their objectives are achieved. This pursuit does not take the form of drudgery as with the nose-to-the-grindstone workaholic however but is a journey of enjoyment. True entrepreneurs have an unusually high level of interest, energy and enthusiasm for everything they do. One dynamic, self-made entrepreneur I interviewed, Bob Casperian, described himself as having "a lust for life" and "a thorough enjoyment of whatever I do". Another outstanding achiever studied by education specialist Benjamin Bloom commented: "You do it because it's fun...you cannot make yourself work hard...you just have to be fascinated by what you do". You will *never*, repeat, *never* go far until you become involved in something you genuinely enjoy.

A passionate interest

This is frequently reflected in an overriding passion, even obsession, for what they do. Over and over among high achievers I have heard them state, "For me, work is play." This is why we so often read reports about entrepreneurs proclaiming that they "have little interest in taking a vacation". Why should they? Their work is their love. They are having fun. There is no wish to "vacate" or escape from something you are enjoying. The entrepreneur's whole energy thrust, heart and soul, is in the task at hand. Why ever *would* anyone want to run off and traipse through museum after museum or lie idle on a hot beach when they are doing exactly what they want to do and enjoy doing?

Many entrepreneurs do of course take vacations but it is at a time of their choice and most likely to be when they are in-between projects. Unless of course they succumb to pressures from others, with the expected result of frustration and feeling miserable.

"This is all very well and good", you say, "but what about me? How am I to find my life's love, the entrepreneurial niche that will set me aflame and make each day a blaze of directed energy, commitment and riches? How do I find the lifework that will wipe out once and for all the inertia, the doubts and the lackadaisical attitude which holds me back?"

Single-minded purpose

You need to understand that there are many paths, any number of which can take you where you want to go. Already you have an inkling, if not a strong notion of this. Few of us lack for ideas and things we enjoy doing. The biggest challenge lies in pulling everything together and arranging your time such that you minimize conflicts between your varied interests and important needs. To tuck away all the distracting influences as you discover your direction, you must have confidence that you are on the right track and also meeting the rest of your responsibilities in life. It is nigh impossible to give your whole self over to entrepreneurial pursuits if you have nagging doubts about what you are doing or if your mind is constantly bombarded with other duties and obligations.

You can only do one thing at a time and do it well. This is so vital to your success, please read it again. *You can only do one thing at a time and do it well.* In order to move up to high levels of success you want to learn how to give your undivided attention to the project at hand. Settle in your mind now any remnants of other priorities battling for your attention by completing the following exercises.

Time Block No. 7
Conflict-Free Living

Get out a sheet of paper and follow the instructions given in the five steps below. It will take you only a few minutes, and start you on the way toward building a stable basis for your pursuits.

Step One:

Itemize the important areas of your life. For example, these might be:

A. Health and fitness
B. Spiritual growth
C. Family and friends
D. Educational growth
E. Recreation and relaxation

Keep your list limited to no more than seven categories. Group as many items together as possible. *Do this now.*

Step Two:

Weight each category according to how essential you perceive it to be for your overall well-being. Do this by writing a number from "1" to "5" with "5" being high, after each category. Thus, if having good family relationships is most important to you at this point in time, put a "5" after it. What is least important? Place a "1" after the category for which you have the least interest relative to the others. Continue this procedure for all the categories you have listed.

Step Three:

Take a good look at your life over the past month and come up with a realistic assessment of the percentage of time you have spent in each area. A sample list is given below.

(A)Health and fitness (jogging, biking, stretching) (10%)

(B)Spiritual growth (attending inspiring lectures, reading New Age literature, having discussions about life's meaning) (5%)

(C)Family and friends (interfacing at home, social engagements and other occasions) (30%)

(D)Educational growth (taking a computer class, learning a foreign language) (20%)

(E)Recreation and relaxation (going to the movies, resting) (40%)

As you begin to think about the activities filling up your days and evenings, you will notice that there are several items which may overlap the different categories. For instance, you go to the movies with a friend. Should you include this under "C" or

"E"? The answer is both. Your total percentages then can add up to over 100%. Or, depending on the amount of time you are still putting in on a job, they could drop well below 100%. The point of this exercise is to help you ascertain relative weightings for clarifying the priorities in your life and how these are impacting on current time usage.

To simplify matters in estimating percentages, think in terms of having 100 waking hours per week available. That would be roughly 15 hours per day, 7 days a week. Then just mentally add up the approximate hours you have been spending in each category. Although this is a rough indicator of time use, it is guaranteed to give you valuable insights on how your time is being proportioned. If you feel more ambitious, use a daily time log over the next few weeks and actually keep track of your minutes and hours. This will furnish you with a more accurate representation. Of greater importance for now, however, is to get something down on paper to work with. It can be corrected and updated as you go along.

Step Four:

After you have all the percentages filled in for each category, take a look at how your priorities match up with your time use. Where is the bulk of your time being spent and how does this relate to your objectives? What changes come to mind?

Step Five:

You'll notice that up to this point in the exercise I have made no mention of time allocation for entrepreneurial projects or financial independence. Did you include this as one of your categories? If so, how did it rate in Step Two and Step Three?

Did you rate it a number "5", of top importance? How does entrepreneurship fare on current time usage relative to the other categories you have listed?

If you neglected to list entrepreneurship or any creative endeavors on your list, or assigned it a low ranking, you need to go back to Chapter Two and reassess the value of entrepreneurship and financial independence in your life. *Picture the creative enterprise as the core of your existence.* As your purpose unfolds within the temporal sphere, specific entrepreneurial projects and financial independence come to engulf your life. This in turn makes possible the fulfillment of other important dimensions: for example, bountiful health and fitness, true friendship and loving relationships. (See Figure 4)

Philosophers and psychologists have portrayed the human condition and our hierarchy of need development in a variety of ways. I do not visualize it as a hierarchy at all, but more as a conscious, choiceful unfolding and leafing off process. A feedback mechanism from each aspect of the external environment operates throughout the creative plane of your existence. As the creative force expands within your time frame, the experience of life is enriched, and blossoms forth for you like a flower from a bud.

The previous four steps of this exercise were designed to help you assess the current status of the significant elements interplaying on your time. Now you are to take a mind-step toward reordering your priorities in tune with your creative mission. It doesn't matter whether you have figured out what your enterprise is yet. Discovering your purpose within the creative realm will give you direction and vitality. And as your visual map of this phenomenon becomes more crystalized, each of the scattered segments of your life start falling easily and

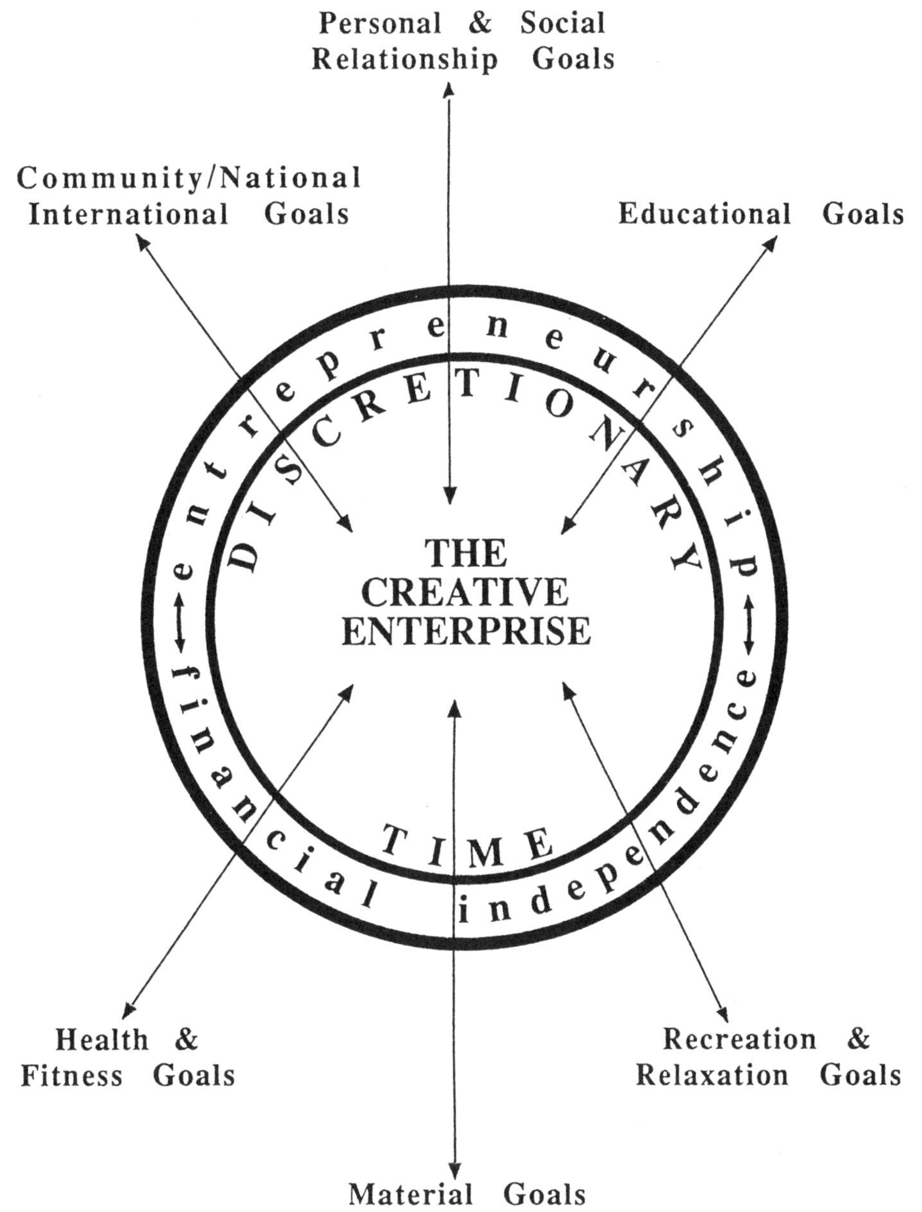

Figure 4: The Interplay Between Creativity, Time and Entrepreneurship

naturally into place. Have patience. Each small step you take will let you glimpse a clearer picture of where you are going.

Summary of Steps

Step 1. Itemize the important areas of your life.
Step 2. Weight each category.
Step 3. Estimate the percentage of time spent in each area.
Step 4. Check priority and time match.
Step 5. Evaluate entrepreneurship and time use.

Time Block No. 8
Mind Bolstering

Set aside one hour at the beginning of each week, either Sunday or Monday morning, to bolster your mind state toward the entrepreneurial pursuit. With respect to other important dimensions of your life, here are some insights and guidelines to follow:

Health and fitness

Observe a sound diet and exercise program to keep your energy level up and to ward off disease. Remember, your goal is to keep your body in shape to support your creative mission and purpose in life. Don't get carried away with time-consuming health fads and crazes such as running marathons, doing triathalons and cross country biking. There will be plenty of time for these kinds of activities later. Right now you are focusing on the creative enterprise and financial independence. Your objective is to *maintain* your health and physical well-being, not become a super athlete.

Spiritual growth

Taking a look at your value system, determine the functions and activities you want to participate in. Make your decision based on what is right for you without pressures from others. Decide on a minimum amount of time to spend here and still keep peace with yourself. What you are likely to discover is that your creative mission and spiritual growth will coincide. Though this is not always evident immediately, it will become more obvious as you progress.

Educational growth

Instead of a hodgepodge of miscellaneous information and knowledge that we typically get caught up in, your learning experiences are to center around your creative enterprise. You may need background courses in accounting, computer training or any number of skills. Be guided by your primary interests. If you are presently taking classes or training, reassess their value to you in view of your new direction. Don't however make the mistake of using this as an excuse to quit what you're doing. It is almost always best to finish what you start before going on to something else. If you are honest with yourself and keep your objectives in mind, you can be trusted to make the right decisions.

Recreation and relaxation

Once you get involved in creative endeavors that are an outflow of your personality and interests, you will find yourself losing interest in idle social functions. Excessive drinking and smoking to unwind will be a thing of the past. Your relaxation and restoration will mostly come from quiet moments with good friends or special interests such as golfing, biking and running or nature walks that act to clear the mind and keep you alert and energized.

Family and friends

Here is where most of us get into trouble. Unless you have a spouse or sweetheart who is fully supportive of your entrepreneurial goals, this is going to be a source of friction. It needs to be dealt with immediately.

Recognize that no matter how dedicated, terrific or loving you are, support from others is not going to always be there. Sometimes those close to you will be understanding and allow you the space to do as you have decided is best. On other occasions your time will be demanded and you can easily be thrown off track if you allow it. Handle this by acknowledging and accepting others needs as they occur. At the same time, be firm about your goal commitments and the hours you are blocking out for this purpose. Without resisting or feeling guilty, simply get on with what you need to do.

Avoid getting pulled into feelings of resentment and anger when your loved ones are unable to understand why or what you are doing and do not share your enthusiasm and excitement. Each person is acting as best they know how at any given moment. It is futile and just plain silly to waste time judging them or having any ill feelings about their behavior patterns. As a preventative measure, discuss your entrepreneurial objectives, time requirements and values openly and honestly with the significant others in your life. Explain to them as effectively as you can the importance of your projects to you. Nevertheless, don't expect total approval, appreciation or support. Realize that having the approval and support of others is unnecessary for you to accomplish what you need to do in order to be successful.

We all love approval and pats on the back, especially when we have put in many long hours on a project. And it is easy to fall prey to a "poor me" mind state when appreciation is not forthcoming. Settle this with yourself now to help ward off these feelings getting in the way later on.

Spend the hour you have set aside at the beginning of the week to think through your special situation and any changes you need to begin incorporating in the different dimensions of your life. Come to grips with interpersonal disharmonies and family problems threatening your new lifestyle and reaffirm to yourself the value of entrepreneurship. Don't expect all to go smoothly or be perfect on the homefront at the onset—or ever for that matter. Only stay with your commitment and as you go along you will learn improved living practices that embrace the path you have chosen.

Eleven inspirational messages are provided on the next page to boost your spirit and help keep you on target. Read them aloud, and make them a part of your daily self-talk.

Inspirational Messages

(1)The best plans remain only daydreams until you bring them to life through action.

(2)Dreading a task can be more tiring than doing it.

(3)You cannot get anywhere today if you are still tied down in yesterday.

(4)He who expects nothing shall never be disappointed.

(5)A mistake is evidence that someone tried to do something.

(6)Winners never quit, but quitters never win.

(7)To stand in the midst of darkness and behave as if all is light, that is victory.

(8)Resisting adversity causes some people to break, others to break records.

(9)Smart people speak from experience. Smarter people sometimes don't speak.

(10)If you can't do everything, do everything you can.

(11)In the presence of trouble some people buy crutches, others grow wings.

Nonstructured Time & The Creative Enterprise On-Going Time Blocks

Time Block No. 8 Mind-Bolstering

Set aside one hour at the beginning of each week (Sunday or Monday morning) to bolster your mind state toward the entrepreneurial pursuit.

During this time, resolve any interpersonal disharmonies, or other problems adversely affecting your creative mission and entrepreneurship.

Commit to memory the eleven inspirational messages as an aid for self-support when you need it.

Block this time out in your calendar now!

5
Selecting Your Personal Play Projects

There is one quality more important than 'know-how'... This is 'know-what' by which we determine not only how to accomplish our purposes, but what our purposes are to be."

—NORBERT WIENER

Your Personal Play Projects (PPP) are what you discover to be the best ways to express your individual uniqueness. They are what you truly *want* to devote the bulk of your time and energy to. It might be the development of an innovative product or some modification on an already existing product. It could be a special service that you perform for others. Or it may be neither a product nor a service but something related to marketing and promotion. Examples include designing a new advertising campaign, co-ordinating functions for meeting planners, and revamping a sales program for retail merchants.

In the past we have centered our attention on becoming educated, trained and groomed for a career and spending the biggest part of our lives there. Through our occupations we aspired to release our creative juices, find challenge, meaning and fulfillment. As the disillusion and disenchantment of this mission has become more evident, occupation is beginning to be viewed more as a means-to-an-end. We will get our 9-to-5 out of the way and do what we really enjoy during evening hours, on weekends, holidays and over vacation.

On our own time we ski, sail, swim, attend self-enrichment seminars, dabble in the arts, listen to music and think about all the things we'd like to be doing. We have begun setting up more and more periphery goals around the career, sometimes wishing that we could earn money doing what we enjoy most, but never letting ourselves get too serious about it so long as we are still trudging along in our career fantasies. For most of us, the idea of turning our hobbies and special interests into dollars as a business venture has either remained in the idle, day-dreaming stage or we have made only half-hearted attempts without taking the action steps necessary to get us off the ground floor.

Now, with the time ripe to give our occupations a gentle shove into the background, we can look more closely and more seriously at our predominant interests and learn how to restructure our lives to support them. Only you can determine where your special interests lie. Your PPP or primary interest in life is an expression of your unique personality. Perhaps you have already figured out what you would like to do, but have doubts about your capabilities and if you are making a smart decision. Or you may have a number of different ideas and are unsure about which to explore first and what would work out best for you.

How do you go about selecting the right projects without getting off on the wrong track and wasting good time and energy? Traditionally, entrepreneurs have looked to their background of education, experience, training and what they seemed to have a natural talent for. These were then considered in conjunction with market needs. The question was posed: "What kind of product or service am I qualified to provide that will fill a need in my community, country or the world today?"

Rather than approach this important decision in the usual way, let's view it from another angle. Just as you may have gotten locked into an inappropriate profession or job structure, your past education and training may not be applicable to what is right for you today. We see instances of this all around us. As a young child, Megan enjoyed playing with dolls and acting out the role of nurse. She decided to major in nursing, only to find out many years later that there was a huge gap between what she imagined went along with being a nurse and the stark reality of the profession. She is now working toward a degree in business.

Pretty and talented Lori entered college at the tender age of sixteen. Majoring in fine arts and being a dress designer sounded like fun to her then. Now at age twenty-seven, her interests have completely shifted and she is considering the field of biochemistry.

A number of studies have shown that better than seventy per cent of sons enter the same occupation or a closely related field of their fathers. As more women join the workforce, we see a similar pattern emerging. In many cases, this has come about as a result of pressure from parents, ease of entering and having contacts there, rather than by personal preference.

Far too many people wind up going through years of training and education in a field that is incompatible with their personalities, major interests and desires. Perhaps you have some inkling of what you would like to do as an entrepreneur, however, have rejected your ideas, not due to lack of interest, but because you felt underqualified or were unsure about how to get started. For the moment, forget your past training and think about what you genuinely *want* to do. For high success in any field of endeavor, you need to discover those interests and activities that pose a challenge, something you can become excited enough about to whet your appetite and stimulate your imagination. Having a strong curiosity and interest is far more important than your present qualifications. Information can be obtained and skills can be learned.

It may well be that your PPP will turn out to be just that endeavor which is *the most difficult for you,* the antithesis of your present inclinations and what you have been formally educated and trained for. This poses the biggest challenge of all, and fused with the power of desire, many persons have made miraculous achievements through devoting their time and lives to projects that were the toughest for them personally to master.

To cite just a few examples: Diane, a middle-aged woman determined to conquer her fear of flying, now holds a commercial pilot's license and gives flying lessons to other women. Although she has a doctorate in sociology, and there have been many achievements in her life, she is more thrilled with her flying conquest than anything else.

Rex, formerly a heavy chain smoker, is now running a lucrative stop-smoking clinic. Besides having the satisfaction of kicking a bad habit, he found out how to capitalize on it.

Darren, who used to get tongue-tied talking in front of an audience of three, embarked on giving public seminars and now speaks confidently in front of three hundred people. He has so much fun and enthusiasm talking in front of a group, men and women from all walks of life are flocking to his sessions and paying top dollar.

Advisors to entrepreneurs often emphasize going to the marketplace as a starting point to discover where the predominant needs are, what products or services are "hot" at the moment, and what the competition looks like. While you do not want to be oblivious to market needs, there are several problems with assuming this posture. First, the needs of the public can be quite fickle, changing almost overnight. What is in hot demand in the marketplace today may be obsolete tomorrow. If I listed specific products that are booming now, by the time you read this and got yours underway, it could be a dying industry.

Many seminars and information sources for the entrepreneur have sprouted over the last decade promising million dollar money makers. There is nothing wrong with these ideas *if* you can get fired up enough about one of them, not only during a Saturday pep rally, but for the time period it takes to get it accomplished. And this is going to depend on nothing less than *your* personality and passionate, sustained interest. Generally speaking, you will have greater enthusiasm and motivation for those projects you've discovered on your own.

Another problem with approaching prosperity from this stance is that it often proves to be short-sighted. If anything, you want to know what market needs will be tomorrow, down the road a bit, not today. It is also quite possible that your Personal Play Project is just the thing to help create a needed, but yet unknown product or service. Again, it will be said by hard-nosed market followers and dollar chasers that "if the market isn't currently there, forget it". While this contained some truth in the past when we had limited media communication resources, it no longer holds up. With instant access to millions of people through television, computer satellite and the press, a new market can be created practically overnight. Witness the pet rock, teddybear and cabbage-patch doll crazes.

Certainly you do not want to be so far removed from today's market and reality that you specialize in something as future remote as wrist-wallets for women traveling about the moon. Even this, however, would not be the gravest of mistakes if you enjoyed doing it and were prepared for the financial consequences. And with a wealth consciousness, such an item could make money in spite of its lack of utility. A more prevalent mistake and risk is to focus exclusively on market needs without considering (perhaps never knowing) what *you* want to do—what your unique personality lends itself to.

Insofar as you act within your own lights, even when you make mistakes and things fail to go as planned, the time spent will not have been wasted. To the extent that you are doing your best, the process has been worthwhile, and you can correct for mistakes the next time around. If on the other hand you are always attempting to put out what you think the other guy wants in order to make a fast buck without regard for what you feel good about, you are not only likely to be devastated by the failures which eventually will come your way, but may find yourself wondering about your lackluster satisfaction and mixed reactions even when you are able to pull off a financial coup.

If your background of experience and training misses the mark, and doing what's currently in vogue is unsound, what approach are you to use? Where do you begin? In the next pages I am going to give you a seven-step method that shows you how to put your time together so you can discover exactly what money-making entrepreneurial projects are right for your personality. Even if you are already involved in an on-going business, use this method to solidify your commitment and maximize your energy and enthusiasm. ***This approach is guaranteed, and has already helped thousands of people fulfill their dreams, let's go!***

Time Block No. 9
Steps to PPP Discovery & Profit

Set aside six hours this week to complete the following steps. They are best done in three, 2 hour sessions.

Step 1. Free Time Enjoyment Probe

Begin by exploring your secret desires. Is there something you used to enjoy but no longer do? What have you always had a yen for? It doesn't matter how crazy it is if it's what you want to do and is harmless. It might be an artistic achievement, a physical feat or a new learning experience. Perhaps you have always had a secret desire to sing opera, cut a record, act in a local play, try your hand at sculpture, learn belly dancing, study Greek or conduct an orchestra. Does sailing across the Pacific, hang gliding, light plane flying or doing a thiathalon excite you? You may wish to dwell into the new psychophysics, learn navigation, take up snow skiing or swim a mile without stopping.

Lest you start to protest, "What has all this got to do with entrepreneurship and riches? Surely, I'm not going to get rich hang gliding, skiing or belly dancing!" No, perhaps not, but once you identify those activities you especially *want* to do, this will provide the impetus and set the stage for branching out into lucrative dollar domains. This can happen in a variety of ways. Here are a few examples from actual case histories:

A Sacramento neurologist with a passion for snow skiing and little love for his profession has spent the last two winters as an instructor at Alpine Meadows in Tahoe. Since there is little monetary compensation for teaching skiing but the mountains is where he wants to be, Bob has recently become a working partner in a chain of ski shops around the area and is phasing out of his Sacramento medical practice. Because skiing is his primary "love", he knows what skiers like and want, and with his strong desire to succeed, it's highly probable that his business venture will be profitable.

Any number of boating enthusiasts have found their way to profit and fun by providing charter services, instruction, serving yacht owners' maintenance needs and acting as yacht brokers. One artistic boat-minded entrepreneur developed a line of nautical jewelry and can barely keep pace with the orders pouring in.

As far as some of the other off-the-wall activities I've mentioned, consider that dollars—big bucks—have been made at just about everything the human mind is capable of conceiving. Doreen, a young woman who has always loved soft, cuddly teddy bears, opened a store many years ago specializing in just that. Long before the teddy bear craze took hold and branched out to teeshirts, decals, bumper stickers and all the other things entrepreneurs are dreaming up, Doreen took the risk and did what she wanted. Today, this successful Berkeley store with its high profit margin is keeping her as cozy and happy as the teddies she is surrounded by.

Remember how you loved parties and balloons as a child? Putting this together, one opportunity-minded entrepreneur came up with "Balloons for Parties", providing colorful helium balloons for birthdays, weddings, special affairs and other festive occasions. Many since have followed suit.

We see all sorts of catering services and specialty foods originating out of the imaginative tastes of someone's kitchen. Debbie Fields of Mrs. Field's cookies is fond of telling the story about how she loved cooking and eating big soft doughy cookies. Everyone told her she was crazy to think that she could ever go out and sell them, but that was what *she wanted to do.* And she wanted to do it badly enough that she didn't care what anyone thought about it. In three short years she grossed over five million dollars.

Even amateur belly dancers and exhibitionists-strippers have gotten themselves booked at parties and conferences for handsome fees. More enterprising individuals have started a chain of "party-act" services. On a grandiose scale, whoever would have thought that Walt Disney with his crazy mix of fantasy and technology would have made such a hit and financial success? Or Buckminster Fuller with his iconoclastic, futuristic inventions?

A commodity as unlikely as garbage can pay off big. Another entrepreneur with a vision for creating a giant network of sanitary trucks across the nation, rose to multi-millionaire fame in just a few years.

Giving training classes, teaching seminars, and doing consulting on virtually every topic, from laughter lectures to getting rid of hiccups to dealing with fears of dentists, has put fortunes in many pockets. We see big money being made from designing, manufacturing, selling and promoting everything from expensive specialty items to nickel-and-dime trinkets. Fortunes have been made on wooden ducks that sell for $2000 or more each to bags of tropical air that sell for under $2.00.

Don't waste time doubting for a minute then, that once you have clearly identified YOUR special interests, whatever they might be, that you will be able to turn them into dollars. ***It is not the idea, product or service that makes the difference between success and failure, but YOU—the creator.***

The crucial task for the moment is to discover what your unique personality lends itself to. Few of us lack for different things we enjoy, and with an endless array of possibilities tempting us, it's difficult to stay focused. Most clients and persons I talk with have such an overload of desires, wishes and different activities they would like to try, they find themselves scattered in their attempts to do too much.

To help you narrow the scope of your interests, do the exercises given in the following steps and assess where your primary focus is best centered.

Step 2. Cognitive-Imagery Probe

A content analysis of your prevailing thoughts and mental imagery will provide you with insights about your dominant interests and personality. This involves a simple introspective observation of your thought stream. To get started, write down your responses to each of the questions below:

(A)What thoughts continually invade your consciousness?

(B)What do you tend to reflect on most in life?

(C)What do you most often see yourself doing in your mind's eye?

(D)What are your first thoughts when you awaken in the morning?

(E)What are your thoughts as you drift off to sleep?

Next, probe yourself on the kinds of things you are most curious about. Use the list below as a stimulus:

(A)The workings of nature?

(B)How people think and feel and act?

(C)How machines work?

(D)The effects of diet on health and behavior?

(E)Metaphysical issues?

(F)Dreams and sleep behavior?

(G)Are you inspired by music, politics, space phenomena or the mystics?

In the book, ***Free Time,*** (Wiley & Sons, 1983) there are a number of explorations which will help you do a more systematic inventory and analysis of your interests.

Over the next few days keep a log of your recurring thoughts and mental pictures. Use the Cognitive-Imagery Log provided on the next page (See Figure 5). It is important that you penetrate through the surface of your present life patterns and past conditioning to get in touch with those areas that spark your interest and challenge you. What offers a great enough challenge to keep you aroused and on target over all the lesser desires and distractions constantly bombarding you?

SAMPLE DAILY CALENDAR

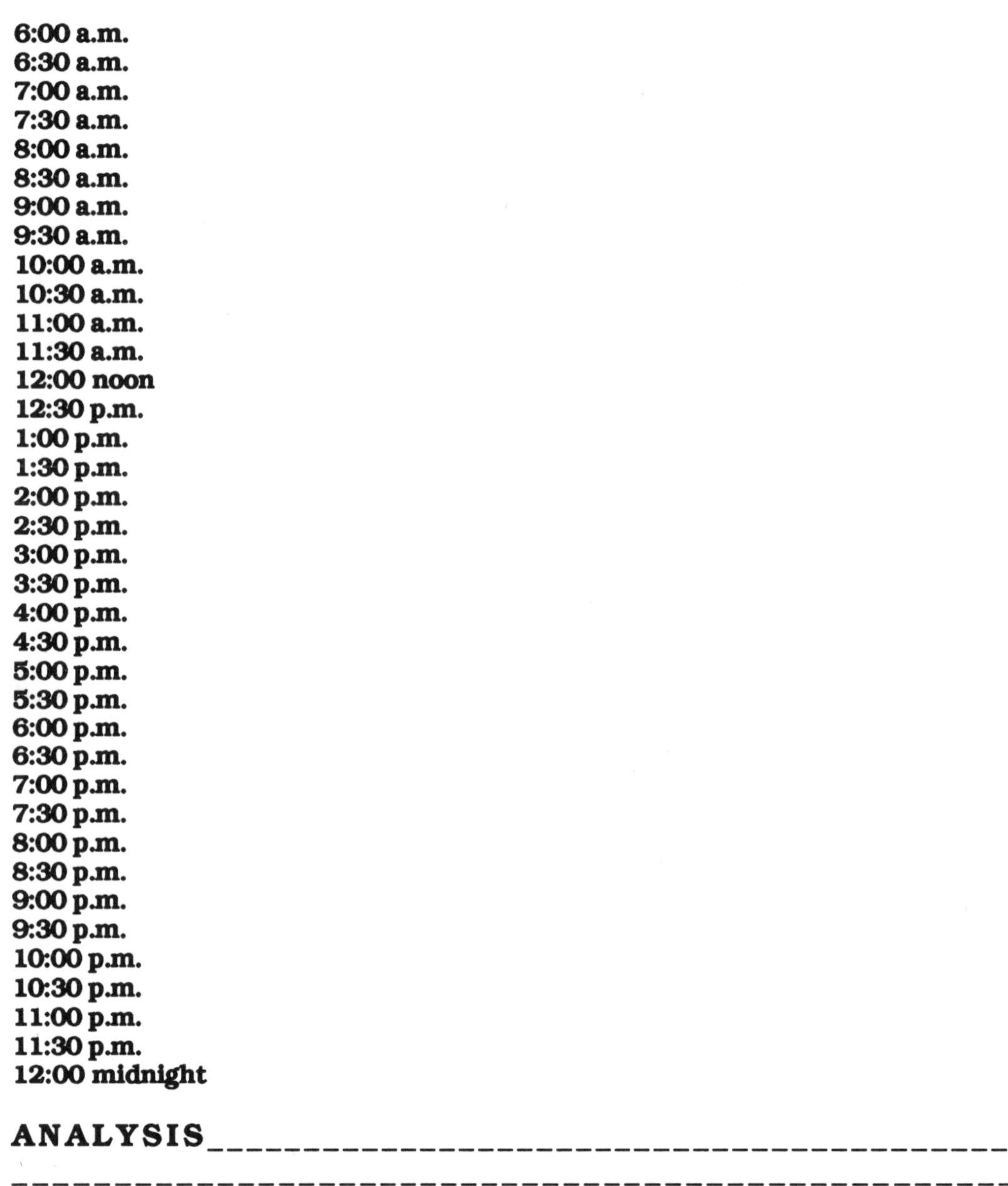

	THOUGHT STREAM	IMAGES
6:00 a.m.		
6:30 a.m.		
7:00 a.m.		
7:30 a.m.		
8:00 a.m.		
8:30 a.m.		
9:00 a.m.		
9:30 a.m.		
10:00 a.m.		
10:30 a.m.		
11:00 a.m.		
11:30 a.m.		
12:00 noon		
12:30 p.m.		
1:00 p.m.		
1:30 p.m.		
2:00 p.m.		
2:30 p.m.		
3:00 p.m.		
3:30 p.m.		
4:00 p.m.		
4:30 p.m.		
5:00 p.m.		
5:30 p.m.		
6:00 p.m.		
6:30 p.m.		
7:00 p.m.		
7:30 p.m.		
8:00 p.m.		
8:30 p.m.		
9:00 p.m.		
9:30 p.m.		
10:00 p.m.		
10:30 p.m.		
11:00 p.m.		
11:30 p.m.		
12:00 midnight		

ANALYSIS ____
____
____

Figure 5: Cognitive-Imagery Log

Step 3. Cosmic Energy Probe

This time, instead of logically trying to figure out where your primary domain of interests lie, I want you to put yourself into a deeply relaxed alpha state and pose some questions to yourself. To enter into this relaxed state, listen to a meditation tape or follow this procedure:

Get into a comfortable position, either sitting or lying down. Breathe in deeply and hold it to the count of 3, then breathe out slowly, again to the count of 3. Do this several times until you feel yourself beginning to relax completely. Clear your mind of any worries, disappointments, past painful experiences and future concerns. Let go and relax.

Now ask yourself: "What would give me the greatest satisfaction and sense of worth and fulfillment?" "Of all the things that I might do with my life, what is it I desire most?"

Reflect on those activities which genuinely give you satisfaction. Sometimes, we think we like a particular activity, but then when we actually do it or consider the effects on us, it isn't what we really want or would choose. For example, many of our recreational and social habits lead us to drink and smoke too much, waste excessive time with people whose company we don't much enjoy, then wake up the next day feeling drained and unfulfilled. Try to identify those hours in your life that have been the most rewarding. What were you doing, thinking and feeling?

Many of us fantasize about starting one of the popular businesses we have patronized: a charming bread and breakfast inn, a sparkling restaurant, a bustling travel agency. Probe your mind for the sentiments coloring your choices. If a travel agency keeps popping into your head, is it because you have visions of bouncing about the continent and staying in exotic places? Does the idea of having your own restaurant appeal to you because of happy moments dining in your favorite place? Let your mind wander and visualize those options which seem right for you.

While you are in this quiet alpha state, also probe the ways in which you are different and special. At a visceral, gut level, what do you hear your innermost being confiding to you? The insightful poet Homer said, "I consulted with my own great soul." Rest assured that you will arrive at an answer to these questions if you dwell on them awhile and play around with any ideas which come up.

As emphasized earlier, your PPPs need not be lofty or grande goals. You may recall how Tolstoy glorified and saw meaning in the daily repetitive activities of the peasant. Only you are in a position to decide what is right for you. As the new entrepreneur you bear the burden and the glory of generating your own rules and playing out your own drama. If fixing up junker houses excites and stimulates you (and it does a good many people) then buying and selling such properties might be just your niche.

Be careful not to toss out your ideas based on past conditioning. For example, in our culture, many of us have learned to denigrate various types of physical labor. Doing housework, carpentry and cleaning are seen as degrading. Yet I have observed quite a number of well-educated and intelligent persons who dearly love working with their hands. One evening while I was sitting in the home of the enthusiastic architect, Richard Clements at Big Sur, California, he confessed, "I get as much excitement and fun out of laying those bricks (out by the deck) or doing carpentry and building that room as I do a big new business enterprise." Some folks love to refinish old furniture, repair broken gadgets, paint houses, do wall papering and other such physical tasks. Housekeeping maid services and repair services have in fact been two businesses which have flourished in recent years. Our cultural conditioning has kept us from doing too many things too long! Figure out what *you* want to do and forget about getting a stamp of approval from anyone else.

Step 4. Crystalize your Activity Probes.

It is time to get specific and crystalize your activity probes. Do this by listing five activity satisfactions. These might be things you have done in the past but were remiss in completing. Or they might be activities you have thought about doing and wanted to pursue but that got abandoned when other obligations came up. Your listings should follow naturally from the previous three steps.

If you draw a blank or still feel uncertain about what you want to do, don't worry about it. *Write something down anyway.* It is important to make a decision and get started. Keep in mind that whatever you decide today is not carved in cement. It can be changed or modified as you go along. We learn by doing. As your skill and knowledge in a particular area increases, if it is right for you, your enjoyment will increase as well. Getting out of limbo and giving your full attention to something, like it or not, acts as an impetus for branching off into more suitable activities.

Step 5. Connect your PPPs to Profits.

Take six minutes and make a list of all the ways in which you can provide a service for others AND make a profit by spending your time in your favorite activities. Some of your interests could be combined in one business. For example, Kevin always loved biking and enjoyed tinkering with broken machinery. He got a special thrill out of figuring out how to put things back together. Remembering all the times as a boy when his bike broke down and there was no service available to fix it, he thought, "Why not open up a bike repair shop in a location where biking is popular?" Acting on his idea, he opened a place in Pacific Grove on the Monterey Peninsula close to the many biking trails, and has had a smashing success.

Ethyl likes nothing better than to talk on the telephone and give advice. She also likes to cook and is a whiz in the kitchen. This ingenious woman has recently started a neighborhood "Call Ethyl" service and charges $1.00 a minute to answer questions about recipes, ingredients, utensils and all phases of cooking and serving food. Since most advice can be given in five minutes or less, people are happy to send her a check for $5.00 to save them time tracking down a recipe or to quickly learn how to prepare a special dish. Newlyweds, single men and women, party hosts and others seek her advice. Ethyl's telephone line has become so busy, she has hired an assistant. At $60.00 for sixty minutes, she's doing fine in the financial department and enjoying every minute of it.

After you have completed your own list of profitable projects, reach a decision on ONE PROJECT and underline it.

Step 6. PPP-Profit Action

Next, figure out five things you can start doing right now, today and throughout the rest of the week to begin your entrepreneurial venture. For example, it might be going to the library to conduct some research, making telephone calls to set up appointments, writing letters, or laying out advertising copy. Keep your list as specific as possible.

Step 7. Follow Through Procedures

Block out the time in your calendar for each of the activities you listed in Step 6. Be careful to block out time for not only the end project goal, but each intervening step that is related to your projects. For instance, if you are going to put on a fund-raiser to obtain capital for your new business, some intervening time blocks could be for telephoning prospective sponsors, drafting invitations, and contacting entertainers.

Block out your first available times for doing the preliminary activities related to your PPP. Here is another example: Your PPP is going to be giving seminars on taking a cruise. Some of the things you need to do are:

(1)Assess the profit potential from similar types of businesses and determine where yours stands. (For example, seminars on vacation planning, traveling abroad, skiing trips)

(2)Sketch out a tentative seminar program.

(3)Check possible sites and costs for holding seminars.

(4)Telephone the sales and catering departments of hotels and ask them to send a packet of information on meeting rooms, services and costs.

(5)Survey the interest of prospective attendees.

It is absolutely crucial that you ***block out time for everything you will be doing concerning your PPP.*** You do not want to just list the end goal six months hence: "Conduct a seminar 10:00 a.m. to 4:00 p.m.". You are to put in each of the *initial and intermediate* action steps toward the completion of the project, viz: Tuesday 9:00 a.m—10:00 a.m.: Request information on meeting rooms from hotels, clubhouses and universities; Wednesday 7:00 p.m.—9:00 p.m.: Draft seminar program.

Always be specific and do not skip blocking in any required activities toward your end goals. These are just the things that will get you bogged down if you neglect scheduling times for them.

You also want to block out two hours in your calendar each week for further planning, assessment and modification of your projects. Be certain to identify a definite period, such as Saturday between 1 and 3 p.m. Remember, if you do not create a time for the important things in your life nothing much is likely to happen.

By now, if you have followed the instructions throughout the book, time blocks should come easy for you. Nothing gives you greater strength than blocking out time and filling it as you have chosen. With each action taken as you have decided you are creating your world. It is the closest step to god power.

Every effort will be rewarded! Your expenditures of creative energy count even when you make mistakes. Know this is so and persevere!

Commit Yourself to Riches

After you have completed the seven steps for selecting your PPP, the next safeguard on your action-success route is to reach a definite decision point that you are going to follow through. If you have seriously pondered your desires and interrogated yourself sufficiently, you have narrowed the scope of your interests considerably. Nevertheless, you probably still have a number of related ideas in mind and need to further refine the details of your venture. For example, suppose you have hit on a hot idea for conducting seminars throughout the United States. You are excited about your seminar topic and anxious to share it with others and cash in. The same topic would lend itself well to a national newsletter. This could also be a big money-maker. You find yourself intrigued by both and are unsure about which to pursue. What should you do? Since the two go hand in hand, perhaps you should do both. Taking steps to carry out one project now, with the thought that you can do the other at a later point in time will keep you from getting stuck in indecision and having misgivings about which is the best choice. You therefore opt for first conducting seminars.

More important than what you do is that you do. And it is the quickest way to break out of a mind impasse. Once you decide on a specific project and give yourself the go-ahead, further choices need to be made. In this case, some of the questions to be addressed are: What audiences shall you target? What are the geographical locations with the greatest potential? What are the best procedures for getting everything rolling smoothly?

At every stage in the implementation of your project, you will be facing dozens of decision points and feeling some uncertainty. Taking an attitude of total commitment gives you the confidence to make the best choice possible in each instance without letting your energy and action get bound up in doubts and confusion.

Your attitude is one of resolute conviction! *"No matter what"* I intend to do this. "I have decided that it is right for me at this particular period in time and nothing under the sun is going to prevent me from achieving my objectives." With this kind of driving force and free energy level directed only in support of your PPP, you cannot help but surmount any difficulties that come your way.

This commitment is to be made strictly to yourself. Only you are the final judge and jury of what is worthy when it comes to your time and life. Announcing your plans to others, unless for some purpose, tends to diffuse your energy level. You have probably noticed that those who are constantly chattering about what they are going to do never get much done. Talking about your goals excessively indicates a bid for approval and support from others, and may suggest doubts about your decision. People who derive satisfaction from simply talking about their ideas are not taking themselves any more seriously than anyone else is likely to take them. In addition, you will find that others are rarely enthusiastic about any ideas originating outside of themselves, and can put a damper on what you wish to do. In starting out as an entrepreneur, be exuberant, but be exuberant alone.

Time Block No. 10
Commitment to Action

Take our your daily calendar and under today's date write in bold letters, "I, _______________________________ (your name), commit myself to _________________________________ (the PPP you have chosen) and riches." If your calendar is not handy, write it out on the margin above along with the date.

Hobbyist or Entrepreneur?

Before turning to the next chapter, the distinction needs to be made between spending one's time as a hobbyist and spending it in pursuit of a money-making enterprise. Looking around you, it's easy to observe those persons who have put in long hours, even years on creative projects they found interesting and are yet to realize any financial gain. You saw an example of this in an earlier chapter with my friend Larry.

There are a number of fundamental differences between the person who is a strict hobbyist and the person with an eye toward financial independence. First of all, many hobbyists tend to be dilettantes, skipping from one endeavor to another without any overall sense of direction and purpose. Dividing time among a number of unrelated activities, their energy becomes dissipated. Hobbyists are void of the passionate dedication and channelization of energy found in the true entrepreneur. There are exceptions to this of course. Certain personalities have the self-discipline to go all out in their pursuit of a project and follow through with excellence regardless of whether there is any financial payoff or tangible reward. The act of completion itself is satisfaction enough.

In our naturally curious, creative state of being, and given enough time and energy, each of us will be drawn to the varied projects and challenges that happen into our paths. And if there is no great need or desire for a dollar return on what we do, it is unlikely that we will get one, regardless of how clever and original we are or what the potential market value might be.

The entrepreneur, on the other hand, has a more comprehensive viewpoint and has thought through his or her wants on all counts. Substantial financial rewards are an expected return for time and effort. The advantages of achieving wealth and structuring time in line with this goal have been well established. There is no reservation or guilt associated with making a lot of money. On the contrary, any guilt would stem from *not* taking care of this essential responsibility. As an entrepreneur, you can be idealistic, dedicated and of the highest integrity, and expect to receive a fat monetary reward from your projects. In the mind of the true entrepreneur these goals are inextricably intertwined and completely compatible.

High success entrepreneurs know that time is money. That's not all it is to be sure, nonetheless, time-as-money is more for them than a hackneyed concept: It is a cornerstone in their self-management. Conversely, hobbyists generally act as if they have all the time in the world and neglect apportioning this commodity consistently. They are challenged by the project of the moment and their habit-activity-pattern continues until something else grabs their attention. Many hobbyists are notorious for incomplete projects. Feelings of low self-esteem and a lack of self-fulfillment are the end result.

Most hobbyists fail to get rich from their endeavors regardless of how much time and effort they expend, except by chance, luck or a fluke. Sometimes, a relative or friend with an entrepreneurial bent will see the market potential in the hobbyist's ideas and become partners with them. More commonly, others are too involved in their own worlds to maintain any special interest in anyone or anything that has yet to prove itself. If an interested party does come along, he or she is likely to capitalize by buying the hobbyist out or developing a similar product.

Typically, hobbyists are so wrapped up in the development of their pet project that they wear blinders concerning its market value. In other instances, they are aware of the dollar potential but do not wish to clutter up their minds with sales and marketing details. "Sales" for many persons has a certain stigma attached to it and these hobbyists will go out of their way to avoid any hint that they are engaged in this nasty activity. Such an attitude is not only a detriment to their financial health but does a disservice to those who need and could benefit from their creation. If you have a valuable or outstanding product and neglect getting the word out and the exposure to make it known to others, the consumer may by necessity be resorting to inferior products.

Keep in mind that the creative entrepreneurial process presupposes a socially useful and desirable product or service. It was not meant to be hidden under a blanket. You have a responsibility to communicate the benefits of your PPPs to others. If marketing and sales is neither your strength nor your interest and you prefer to move on to your next creative endeavor, this is fine. As a serious entrepreneur, however, it is your task to find someone who is capable of handling those areas of the business where you are weak or unmotivated. To be a top entrepreneur you need to be able to *both* target your unique creative challenge *and* figure out how to translate it into consumer desires. Obviously, you cannot do everything yourself and you can only do one thing at a time well. Even when you are involved in the nitty-gritty details of a single phase of your business, however, your vision of the whole undertaking, from idea gem to profit gleanings, needs to be held firmly in mind.

Selecting Your Personal Play Project

Time Block No. 9
Steps to PPP Discovery & Profit
Summary of Steps

Step 1. Free Time Enjoyment Probe
Step 2. Cognitive-Imagery Probe
Step 3. Cosmic Energy Probe
Step 4. Crystalize your Activity Probes
Step 5. Connect your PPPs to Profits
Step 6. PPP-Profit Action
Step 7. Follow through Procedures

On-Going Time Blocks

Spend a minimum of twelve hours per week on activities related to your PPP. Block these times out in your calendar as far in advance as is feasible, i.e., three months, six months or more.

Block this time out in your calendar now!

111
Dynamics of the New Entrepreneur within Today's Leisure Ethic

"Leisure is the most challenging responsibility a (person) can be offered."

—Dr. William Russell

6
A Personal/Business Ethos

"Nothing is at last sacred but the integrity of our own mind. Absolve you to yourself, and you shall have the suffrage of the world."

—EMERSON

As you begin your entrepreneurial projects and set up a new lifestyle, it is imperative to think through a basic code of ethics. This will help you resolve the contradictions and conflicts prominent in our era of changing values and keep you on track in your business dealings. Having a working code of conduct minimizes the uncertainty and stress resulting from the many decisions you are required to make at every turn on the path to success. When you know where you stand in your personal philosophy and business ethics, you are able to act confidently and quickly regardless of how difficult your choices might be.

Very few people have formulated much more than a sketchy ethos for themselves. In our past history, this was not deemed all that necessary. Settled into an occupation, most of us felt comfortable enough taking on the values and standards handed down to us through our family, religion, and culture.

Each day was business as usual, attending to the work at hand, content in the knowledge that we were gainfully employed and providing for ourselves and our families.

I have had attorneys, physicians and business persons from all walks of life tell me that they feel lucky in their professions to not have to grapple with any thorny moral or ideological issues that fall outside the scope of their occupation. The justification for shying away from any comprehensive code of ethics or personal philosophy has been, "I have a worthwhile profession, am serving a need, work hard, and..." it is usually confessed, "I wouldn't know where to begin." In addition, there is a sneaky suspicion that too much reflection on their occupations as they are currently ordered might prove uncomfortable.

Today, with the advent of a surplus of free time, greater choice options and an expanded awareness, it has become nil impossible to hold in check the stampede of moral contradictions arising in our lives. As we shed our occupational-value-identity baggage, we are reaching out for a broader world view on which to hang our entrepreneurial hats.

By stepping back, re-evaluating and re-orienting ourselves from an individual ethos rather than organizing our time around The Career, with those matters that truly make a difference shelved and unresolved, we will both upgrade our personal lifestyles and create new institutions in harmony with them.

Social Guidelines

Social considerations involve making those choices in the act of running your business that do not injure or harm another person or group of people. We are all familiar with the oft repeated Golden Rule of "do unto others as you would have them do unto you". Such plateaus, however, give us little help. First of all, we do not always know what might turn out to be detrimental to another. For example, a generous person who continually gives financial support to a friend in need may be encouraging a dependency and preventing his or her friend from learning to stand on their own two feet.

George Bernard Shaw was one of the first to point out the fallacy of the Golden Rule: my wants and desires may not be equal or equivalent to yours. Nor does "do unto others what you think they would like" hold up because we are often unable to surmise others desires correctly. An all too common mistake is misjudging just what it is others want. Possibly this is because so few of us ourselves know what we want and need. How then could we possibly expect to know what is good for anyone else?

One standard for choice is for you to make your decisions based on your own value system and sense of what is right. As indeterminate as this sounds, if you take the time to consciously think through where you stand in those areas of life where you are actively involved, and are honest with yourself, it is likely that your entrepreneurial choices will reflect this integrity. Mistakes can be corrected as your knowledge and experience grows. If, on the other hand, you willfully choose a dishonest course of action for temporary gain, expediency or whatever reasons, it should be self-evident by now that the greatest harm is going to be to yourself.

The concepts, examples and charts in this chapter are given to assist you in clarifying and expanding your own value system. It will be your responsibility to implement them with respect to your particular business venture.

To get started, follow the six recommendations provided below.

(1)Use Enlightened self-interest

A concept we are learning more about is *enlightened self-interest.* While the majority of us are familiar with the Golden Rule, few people have heard of the Silver Rule as taught by Gina Cerminara, author of *Many Mansions.* It states, "Don't let others do unto you what you would not do unto them." You have the right to act in your own best interests, insofar as your behavior does not violate the rights of others. It is up to you to stand up for what you believe in and want, and refuse to give anyone the power to manipulate, control or coerce you into doing otherwise. The truth is, no one can harm you without your consent: you and only you have dominion over your world, and that includes your perceptions, your actions and your emotional states.

To show you how the Silver Rule can be applied, here are two examples:

You have put your house up for sale to raise some capital for your business. Although you have no previous experience in real estate negotiations, you are attempting to sell it yourself and save on a real estate broker's commission. You have advertised your property in the local newspaper for $150,000 but will be happy with $145,000 and a $20,000 cash down payment. Mr. Thomas, an experienced real estate investor, looks at your home, likes it and makes an offer of $125,000 with $10,000 down. Actually, unbeknown to you, Mr. Thomas believes that $145,000 would be a good price for the property and is prepared to go up to that amount and also put $20,000 down. He is testing the water to get the best price and terms possible. You, however, let your ego get in the way, become insulted at his low offer on your beautiful house and tell him where to get off at. He says "fine" and walks away from the deal. Neither of you get what you want.

Let's look at this same situation a little differently. You have had your house on the market for a while with no offers. Mr. Thomas comes along this time and offers you $125,000 with $10,000 down, exactly as in our previous example. You believe it is worth $145,000 but need the money and are nervous about losing the sale. You tell him he can have it for his price of $125,000 with $20,000 down. Thomas, prepared to pay much more, happily agrees. Two weeks later, after the contracts are signed, you start feeling angry and resentful at Thomas and accuse him of taking unfair advantage of you. In reality, it was *you who set the limits on yourself.* You failed to apply the Silver Rule by giving Thomas the power to purchase your property at a lower price than you really wanted to settle for then shifted the blame to him.

You had every right to come back with a counter offer of $140,000 or $145,000 to his $125,000 *during the negotiations.* Once you have agreed to a price, whether verbally or in writing, you bear the consequences even if it is not what you wanted. It is neither ethical nor mentally healthy to harbor negative emotions and misgivings about a deal that is over and done with.

(2)Keep your agreements

This type of situation comes up frequently in business transactions in one form or another. You agree to sell your used car for $4000.00, the buyer gives you a deposit to hold it, and guess what? A better offer comes along. What do you do? Or you're having a garage sale, a buyer is writing you out a check for $200.00 for that old computer you've been trying to get rid of, and another party offers you $250.00.

How you handle yourself when you have made a bad deal says a lot about you and your value system, and how successful you are destined to become. Instead of learning from the experience and accepting the consequences of mistakes, many people run to an attorney hoping to find some angle in the grey legal maze, place the blame on the other party and bail themselves out. And the more money at stake, the more self-righteous justifications they are likely to tell themselves. Such actions rarely lead to financial rewards for anyone except the attorneys contracted. At your expense, attorneys are delighted to spend hours searching for every conceivable interpretation of a transaction that might be blown up, distorted and viewed as a misrepresentation. And if they can get you fired up enough about what "has been done to you" to file a lawsuit, their wallets get even fatter.

(3)Face up to your mistakes

It has been my experience in dealing with both very successful, affluent persons and those who continually fail (in life and in business) that in practically every instance, it is the latter who keep the army of attorneys in business and themselves broke. When you do not do as well as you would like in a business dealing or make a mistake, learn to face it squarely, evaluate how you can improve the next time around, then forget it and go on to the next project. Expending time and energy on your mistakes, attempting to punish others and avenge yourself is just the thing that will halt your progress. No matter how self-righteous you feel or believe that someone has treated you unfairly, placing blame and seeking revenge are surefire routes to failure. The occasional money that you collect through lawsuits, fuming and making trouble for others is *simply not worth it and damaging to your wealth consciousness.*

(4)Determine your negotiating style

Practically every kind of business requires making use of negotiating strategies at one time or another. Most instruction we find here takes the form of showing you how to press your advantage to get the best bargain, best price, best deal or in some way be "one up" on the other party. There are, however, other approaches to take. What I'd like you to strive for is a threefold strategy. First of all it should be consistent with your own code of ethics. Secondly, you want it to make sense business wise. Finally, it should lend itself to your particular personality. Being aggressive and always pushing for your advantage over the other party may not fit your personal style. A "softer" approach to business might be more appropriate.

Let's go back to our real estate example and view it from the other side of the coin. This time we will hypothesize that *you* are the experienced real estate investor, and brilliant at negotiating the best possible deals for yourself. On the other hand, you have thought through your code of ethics and have a policy whereby you believe that both parties in a business liaison should wind up with an agreement in which they are mutually satisfied. Thus, rather than always pressing your advantage and getting the best possible deal for yourself, you take into account the needs of the other person along with your own. For instance, in the above example, after the seller has reluctantly agreed to a price of $125,000 you might ask them again, "Are you certain that you are going to be satisfied with this?" In other words, you give them an opportunity during the negotiations to back down if they are feeling uneasy about the deal. Or you might have initially offered them a figure closer to the asking price. From this ethical stance, you may not always get as much as you are capable of negotiating for yourself in any one circumstance, nevertheless, acting within your value system, you have built up a reputation of being very fair in your transactions, people trust you and business is brisk. Such a policy becomes self-reinforcing.

This is not to say that other kinds of negotiating tactics are wrong or bad. In our earlier example, Mr. Thomas's moral position may have been stated along such lines as these: "I studied and worked hard to learn the business and the best negotiating tactics possible. If you are going to conduct business, it is your responsibility to do the same, and until you do to bear the consequences of your mistakes". Whose attitude and strategy is more moral isn't the issue. What I am proposing is that you take time to figure out where *you* personally stand.

(5)Take stock of your personal/business tactics

Reflect on the way you have been handling your particular set of circumstances and assess whether it is in keeping with your own ethical framework. The first step of course is to *have* a code of conduct. By bringing the personal and business tactics you habitually use into your conscious awareness, you are in a position to more objectively appraise them.

Observe yourself under a variety of conditions both at home and at work. Suppose that you borrow a friend's car and scratch the door driving too close to a tree. Do you face up to what happened and accept responsibility or do you attempt to rationalize it away? Do you place the blame elsewhere when something happens that you don't want to deal with? "Someone at the shopping center must have banged their door into the car while I was out shopping".

It is easy for us to see irresponsible patterns in the behavior of others, especially our friends and relatives. We see how

Mary never admits to a mistake or error of judgment, but always finds a way to place the blame on others. Or Dora, who readily admits forgetting to mail an important letter for you, but is quick to attack you for bringing it to her attention. Then there is Sandie who is always borrowing your clothes to inevitably spill something on them and keeps "forgetting to bring them back" when they're actually at the cleaners.

We can clearly see the fabrications, excuses and foolish habits of those around us. It is not so easy to admit to our own. You will find that the closer you strive to maintain a consistency between your values and your actual behavior, the fewer internal conflicts, self-reprisals, anxiety and guilt you'll have, and as a result, less wasted time and greater financial gain. As you become a better observer of your present automatic behaviors and the values they represent, you will discover changes you can make that are increasingly consistent with your conscious choices.

If you are of a mind to conduct business like our example of Mr. Thomas, taking a tough stance, be sure you are on a solid foundation and emotionally equipped to deal with the envious and the avenger seekers. Also, understand that no matter how high your personal integrity, honesty and fair play in business dealings, there will always be a few people out there who are going to be disgruntled, fault-finders and trouble-makers. I have known some high success entrepreneurs bend over backwards to be fair and still get burned on occasion. You are not responsible for other people's misdoings and can only go so far in your efforts to make concessions and appease them.

Be cognizant of some basic principles of psychology in your interpersonal affairs. For instance, most people tend to project on others their own personality shortcomings. If a person is untrustworthy and devious, he suspects everybody else is also.

To keep your own mental balance, be as clear as possible about what you believe in and govern yourself accordingly. An ill-thought-out, sloppy code of ethics met with reflexive behavior according to the whims and pressures of the moment might make you money on occasion in your entrepreneurial pursuits, but is guaranteed to keep you emotionally on edge, and be overall unprofitable.

(6)Establish ethical policies & practices

Many would-be entrepreneurs I have counseled have told me that they have walked away from the business world because they "cannot stomach all you have to put up with and take from others". This makes little sense. Unless you are planning to become a recluse, there are going to be rough periods and difficult decisions to make in your life whether in business or out. As an entrepreneur, however, the choices are magnified, and if you are serious about making it, there can be no muddling along. If you become involved in an enterprise which you thoroughly enjoy and have resolved the moral issues so that you are acting with a clear conscience, you will find it much easier to be emotionally free from upsetting circumstances and trouble-makers.

You will also find it easier if you hold an empathic tolerance toward others and genuinely care about their needs. Even when people are unreasonable or use tactics you deem unjust, you can make the choice to harbor no malice or ill-will. What others do after all is their problem and they will pay the price. When you have established a solid ideological foundation for yourself, it is easier to maintain a prosperous emotional posture. Without this, the road to success is rough indeed.

Let's look at an example relevant to many businesses: policies on refunds. Early in my consulting practice in San Francisco, a woman made an appointment, paid the fee for services in advance, and two weeks later telephoned to cancel. She told me that she had decided not to come in for consultations and wanted a full refund. Although she had signed up and paid for three hours on "how to use your time more effectively", she was now informing me that "she didn't have any trouble managing her time". On the contrary, this was a person whom I knew personally to piddle away enormous amounts of time and would benefit greatly from the consultations. I therefore felt justified in refusing her a refund, knowing that once she took the training, she would be delighted and grateful.

While this was quite logical reasoning on my part, it nonetheless violated a basic ethical code which I later realized needed to be put into practice: each person has an inherent right to choose his or her own course of action. I had no right to impose my will on her and in effect demand that she learn how to use her time more effectively, no matter how badly she needed help.

On the other hand, I could have had a "no refund" policy, period, regardless of the reasons given, based on the sound ethical position that each of us is responsible for our agreements and if we fail to carry them out, deserve to bear the consequences, whether that results in loss of money or whatever. While this policy is closest to my own code of ethics, I have found that a strict adherence to such a practice is largely unworkable in today's business world. Instead, I have adopted a "full refund, no questions asked" policy for any dissatisfaction with products or services, and charge only a small cancellation fee for any services unrendered. This position I have observed builds trust and profits. I have also noticed that it is a policy adopted by some of the most profitable firms.

I cite this example so that you can scrutinize your own thought processes and business dealings more closely. Recognize that justifying your position and always "being right" in your interactions with clients and customers is rarely the wisest business practice. When you are faced with two possible policies, neither of which violates your personal code, elect the one that is best for business. When someone fails to keep an agreement with you such as in the above instance, it is not your role to punish them or teach them a lesson. All too often we get sidetracked from our primary business objectives by directing our energy in retaliatory thoughts and measures.

If it is any consolation, you might want to note as I have that those persons who fail to keep their agreements or take unfair advantage, with the exception of unusual circumstances, are generally unsuccessful. Success-oriented persons keep their agreements and appointments. This is reflected in small matters as well as matters of more consequence. They respect others' time and are rarely late (or early) for appointments. In my consulting practice, I have observed that those clients who are the worst time-abusers and the least successful, are just the ones who have no respect for the hour. They will show up sometimes fifteen minutes early and at another time be ten minutes late. On other occasions they call up at the last minute and reschedule.

Hypothetically think through your business or prospective business activities in detail. Try to get a vision of the consequences of your choices. Let's say you are marketing a product valued at $500.00 and have advertised a full warranty to cover any defects that occur within six months of purchase. One of your customers calls up six months and one day after receiving the product and tells you there is a malfunction. You estimate the cost of repair to be about $100.00. Are you going to take a firm position according to the exact terms of the contract and require the customer to pay the cost of repair? Or will you be flexible and pay a portion of the cost? Should you pick up the whole cost? Which is the better policy from both an ethical and business standpoint?

What about other variations on this same problem? Say, defects in one of your products surface three to five days after the warranty expires? Or, the customer is a big account and has a lot of clout? What about a small customer who probably won't buy again regardless of what you do? Do you treat him or her differently? Suppose it is an irate customer who calls up your office using abusive language to your secretary?

Will your response to the situation be governed by such factors as who the customer is, his status or influence? Will your actions be determined by how the customer or client conducted himself in reporting the malfunction? Or will you handle the situation according to how you happen to feel at the moment?

In your business dealings you are going to be confronted with dozens of such choices. Without a basic code of conduct to guide you, you will find yourself floundering in indecision, wasting time, having disgruntled customers and little peace of mind. You'll wind up solving variations of the same basic problem over and over.

Your objective in developing a business ethos is not to have a lot of hard and fast rules, but to have well-formulated guidelines which allow you the flexibility to respond in good conscience and good business to all of the unexpected daily problems and opportunities.

In developing your personal code of ethics, be clear about one factor at the onset: Your ethos needs to be a function of your own frame of reference, and not based on what someone else is doing or not doing to you. When you have established your own internal value system, others' attitudes and actions will have little impact on your choices. The Time Block Exercise on the next page will help you further in formulating your personal and business ethos.

Time Block No. 11
Ethos Clarification

Set aside forty-five minutes and write out a list of your general values. State these in the form of personal affirmations using the list below as a guide. Do this now or at the first opportunity *this week*.

(1)I treat each person, no matter what race, sex or status, with respect and dignity.
(2)I am nonevaluative, noncritical and refrain from judging others, recognizing that each person is responsible for their thoughts, feelings and actions. There is no room for blame in my day.
(3)I am honest in my business dealings and avoid making misrepresentations.
(4)I am a good listener and sensitive to the other person's needs and point of view. I understand that by helping others to get what they want, I help myself get what I want.
(5)I always keep my word to others, or under circumstances where that is impossible, I immediately do what I can to make amends.
(6)I carry out my daily activities in a manner that is harmless to those around me.
(7)I interact with others according to the dictates of my own value system irrespective of their misconduct or unfair treatment of me.
(8)I am respectful of others' time and avoid taking advantage of their minutes and hours by being late or early for appointments.
(9)I do not need to take advantage of someone else's misfortune in order to succeed.

Add to your list as you go along. Sometimes we do not know how we would react in a given situation until we are tested. We all learn from experience and trial and error to a certain extent. Experience, however, is generally the hardest teacher. To get off on the right foot in your business you definitely will find it to your advantage to clarify the code of conduct you intend to adhere to, and be consistent in its application. Use whatever information that you currently have to get started. This can always be refined later. The **Ethos Polarity Chart** provided at the end of the chapter will also help you in determining your strengths and weaknesses.

We turn now to a key standard in your successful interaction with others. It has been alluded to at several points and is so vital to your business dealings, I have put the following section together to amplify and elucidate its messages.

Mental tuning for "acceptance"

In our complex contemporary society virtually every business enterprise requires interpersonal know-how. Many books and articles have been written on how to be a super sales person and influence others. There is only one basic standard of conduct however which you need to learn and practice in order to be highly successful.

First of all, forget about trying to memorize a bunch of rules on how to persuade, manipulate and have your way with others. Such tactics put you in the wrong state of mind and throw you off course. Far too much has been written about the ABC's of doing to others and obtaining a specific result. Rid yourself of all the conflicting information you have read on how to get the upper hand by physically posturing yourself a certain way, dressing in the proper attire and phrasing yourself appropriately. Certainly all of these influence aids have their place, but they miss the most important component.

What you want to do is very simple, though paradoxically difficult until you break out of ineffective past habit patterns. Here it is: cultivate an attitude of acceptance, allowing others to be and act according to their own conscience. Recognize that each person has the right to believe, feel and act from their own frame of reference regardless of how alien that might be to your set of values. This does not mean that you must permit them to do injustices to you, take up unnecessary time or otherwise interfere with your life. Remember the Silver Rule.

Nor should another person's ill-conceived behavior influence your own standards of conduct so that you become swallowed up in their unsuccessful stream of existence. Base your business practices on what you are about, irrespective of the circumstances, climate or character of those about you. This will have the added effect, in many instances, of bringing out the best in those around you so that everyone benefits. As Johann von Goethe has observed: "When you treat others as if they were what they ought to be, you help them to become what they are capable of being".

Here are some specific shifts in thought concerning this issue that you are to incorporate:

Eliminate the "eye for an eye" attitude that is ingrained in so many of us.

How often we hear, "If people treat me right and fair, I'll treat them right and fair. If not, then they deserve everything they get." Or, "He lashed out at me. I'll lash out at him." "He hurt me. I'll hurt him back—worse." Stop a moment and think about this kind of response. Is it truly where you want to be morally, to respond in kind, to always "even the score"?

It is not a question of taking a noble or lofty stand. When you free yourself from these trappings, it is the difference between good business and bad business. Seeking revenge, responding with anger and cluttering up your head with resentments will pull you off the path to riches in short order. Virtually everyone out there living and doing anything worthwhile is going to wind up being the target of abusive behavior on occasion. And the higher up the ladder of success you go, the more envy, abuse and misunderstanding you can expect. If you let yourself get drawn into taking the time and energy to respond to every slight and perceived mistreatment, you'll have nothing left for your own endeavors. Seek to maintain the solid stance that comes from keeping your behaviors pro-active rather than reflexive, reactive and retaliatory. Stop giving others the power to distract you from your projects and priorities.

Replace energy-draining ""I've been wronged" circular self-talk that leads nowhere with a quick reappraisal and concrete resolution.

When you are faced with a person who is unreasonable, irrational, unfair, unscrupulous or just plain mean-and-nasty, instead of letting your thoughts get tied up and misspent in negative energy, substitute self-talk such as this: "His/her accusations (actions, interpretations) are in error. I would prefer that he had not said or done such a thing, however, what he thinks and does is his problem and I will refrain from letting it become mine as much as is possible. Assuredly, I am not going to waste my precious minutes by taking time out of a beautiful day to seek revenge, feel angry, hurt or resentful. That would be foolish and detrimental to my success. I will continue to conduct myself as best I can, within my own code of ethics, and those that truly matter will know me by this."

Make the conscious choice to respond to each situation in a manner that is consistent with your overall best interests.

When confronted with a potential trouble-maker, face him squarely, determine your options, make a decision about how you are going to handle the situation, then follow through and forget it.

Perfecting this mode of response takes some practice. Keep your objectives uppermost in your mind at all times and you'll find it easier to apply. You'll also find yourself becoming more sensitive to all the variables at play in any given situation. This in turn will give you greater resiliency and effectiveness.

Forgive yourself when you make mistakes in your dealings with others.

At times, you too will make mistakes in your affairs with people. (A mistake is any form of behavior that is inconsistent with what you would elect to do given your unique value schema.) When this happens, take full responsibility, admit your error without justifications and guilt, make amends and then put it behind you. It is important to deal with any mistakes you make immediately or as soon as is feasible. If nothing can be done to rectify the situation, acknowledge that this is the case and consciously let go of it. Harboring personal guilt is as detrimental to your success as is vengeance directed toward another.

As you go about your business you will find yourself interacting with many persons who have neglected to figure out any personal ethos, and whenever something happens which displeases them, they simply react from old, ingrained habit patterns. Their behavior may take the form of anger, resentment, manipulation or whatever their dominant tendency is at the moment, letting the chips fall where they may. Be aware that their ill-spent conduct is going to cost them the most in the long run.

To prevent yourself from getting caught up in their negative energy field, accept that this is their behavior at this point in time. Acceptance of another does not mean condonance. It is a state of mind which only says, "it is", without judgment or malice. Little is to be gained by being drawn into an angry person's world and taking an adversary position. This will tie up your energy in the wrong place, and do much more harm than good. Let things be and go on about your business.

Now, you may be saying, "This is all very well and good. But I have to protect my interests. I can't let him get away with this or what will he do to me next? I'm not going to be a wimp and get shoved around!" Actually, no one is "getting away with anything" unless you permit them. You can best protect your interests by being true to your own state of mind and values. When you enter into another's negative energy field, you are bound to operate within a very narrow field of responses. A new dyadic entity slips into existence. And it is here where you find conflict, contradictions and competitions of the ego. Although you may sometimes "win the battle", in another respect and far more important way, you can never win.

Shifting to a state of acceptance allows you to be free from these charades. It also lets you be free from damaging self-talk such as, "He's unfair, stupid, biased and just wait until I have a chance to burn him". This sort of thought stream smothers your creative energy and destroys the best of you. You can never be highly successful with a head pumped full of bitter, raging emotions. Your whole thought-thrust needs to be uninterruptedly directed toward your prosperity goals. That means keeping your mind clear from distracting elements.

Someone has said that the path to success is covered with obstacles and problems. The majority of these are interpersonal disharmonies. If every time one of these problems crops up you stop to take care of it, pretty soon your life will be one long string of putting out fires. Soon, your only goal will be to solve the problem at hand and keep above water.

What I'd like you to do instead is embrace a new level of being. Realize that obstacles and problems are what you see when you take your eyes off the important stuff. Don't give power to those persons who would try to wrap you up in their little bundles of problems. Keep your perspective and stay focused on the matters that count. By moving in the right direction you will avoid becoming besieged and buried under the insignificant. This point is so vital to your success, I would like to paint a few pictures for you so that it will stay planted in your memory.

Do you know where the term "small-mindedness" came from? It evolved from someone whose good mind had shriveled up from lack of use; a person who had neglected the best of their mind—their creativity and mission in life and had gotten bogged down attending to trivia. After a while, all that was left was a "small mind", an ugly piece of grey matter, void of soul and wings, lost in its own trappings.

Many of us have a knack for blowing up every disagreeable incident into major proportions. Everywhere we look we see problems. There seems to be no end to all that must be taken care of before we can get on with our lives. We are so busy and involved in whatever happens to come up, it is impossible to do much else. I used to believe that the best way to deal with a problem was to face it head on, giving my full attention to figuring out every possible solution. Needless to say, this response pattern consumed the greater part of my time and energy. I didn't realize then that often the smartest way to confront a problem is to not confront it. Keep a tunnel vision in relation to your goals. Don't keep looking off to the side and concerning yourself with those who would pull you off the path. The biggest trouble-makers are generally those persons who have not figured out their own purpose in life and as they grope along keep stepping on the toes of others. The best thing you can do is just say, "ouch" and keep on walking.

When you understand what another person's behavior stems from, why they think, feel and act as they do, it is fairly easy to pardon them and purge yourself of any malice. Few of us however have such a grasp of human nature. In addition, we are prone to react from antiquated emotional patterns even after we have intellectually got things straight, and "know" how we ought to be responding. There is always a gap or lag between what we need to be doing and what we actually are doing. Many of us spend a lifetime searching for more knowledge or experience to close this gap and remove the inconsistencies and contradictions in our behavior. This is futile, since as soon as we have figured out one response pattern, another unresolved issue will pop up in its place.

The only way out of this quagmire is through acceptance. Accept what you don't know. Allow for the facts that aren't yet in. Knowledge is always only partially complete and your personal experiences give you but a sliver of the whole picture. You cannot know all the factors prompting another's behavior. Let your self-talk take this form: "Alright, this is the way she is feeling and acting at the moment. I may not condone it or understand it or like it, nonetheless, I can make the choice to let it be, period." End your dialogue right there and get on with what needs to be done according to your priorities.

Mastery of this dimension of your life will open up a whole new vista of being. I guarantee that the closer you can bring yourself around to making this shift in your perceptions about what's going on, the more successful you are destined to be. Truly accepting others as they are without having bad feelings will elicit a flow of interaction and communication in the best interests of every one concerned.

Time Block No. 12
Ethos Polarity Chart

The chart on the next page is designed to assist you in determining your ethical polarities. Few of us are totally honest or totally dishonest, but move about somewhere in between as we attend to our personal and business affairs. Using a pencil, draw a line that best represents where you currently stand. Then in pen, draw a line where you would *like* to see yourself. That's a move toward the positive end of the scale folks, not the negative!

Ethos Polarity Chart

positive			**negative**	
100%	75%	50%	25	0%

Positive	Negative
(1)Truthful	Lie whenever it serves my purpose & I can get away with it
(2)Honest	Misrepresent, distort, deceive, scheme
(3)Keep my word & my agreements whether verbal or written	Change my mind if it suits my purpose; can-not be counted on to abide by what I say
(4)Genuinely care about others & their needs	Don't care about others or their needs as long as they buy my goods
(5)Honor & respect the rights of others	Violate the rights of others; disrespectful
(6)Kind, understanding, considerate, empathic	Insensitive to others, wrapped up in my own world
(7)Tolerant/Accepting; recognize that others are what they are and doing their best	Judgmental, disapproving in posture, tone of voice & actions

A Personal/Business Ethos On-Going Time Blocks

Time Block No. 11 Ethos Clarification

Take fifteen minutes each morning before you start your day and repeat out loud the personal value affirmations you have listed. This will serve as a reminder and reinforcement as you go about your business.

Time Block No. 12 Ethos Polarity Chart

Place the **Ethos Polarity Chart** in a conspicuous place and on the first day of each month do a self re-evaluation to check your progress. Spend at least ten minutes on this.

Block these times out in your calendar now!

7
Attitude Shifts & Action Steps

"In the arena of human life the honours and rewards fall to those who show their good qualities in action."

—ARISTOTLE

A critical characteristic of the successful entrepreneur is having an action ideology. You need to have a conscious orientation out of which your action patterns flow automatically without vacillations, conflicts and disruptions. Effective time structuring parallels your decision-making power. To achieve the success and prosperity you merit means learning how to deal quickly and resourcefully at each decision point.

I have underscored the importance of being grounded in a personal ethos: a code of ethics out of which effective action can spring unfettered by all the reflections and ramifications resulting from a clouded worldview. "Should I or shouldn't I?" "What's right and what's wrong?" "Am I making a mistake or not?" This kind of constant back-and-forth banter with yourself acts to tie up your energy and slow you down. When faced with a major decision, you want to take the necessary time for making realistic risk-reward judgments. What you do not want however is to be constantly thrown off by the hundred and one choices you are confronted with daily. Having a solid ideological foundation helps prevent you from drifting off target and being in bedlam every step of the way.

Many intelligent, creative persons are realizing very limited success for two reasons. One, I have already discussed at length: focusing energies on an occupation instead of turning attention toward building riches from a personal nucleus of power. Secondly, are those persons who have developed an expanded consciousness and are capable of performing great feats but have become so ladened with the weight and responsibility of private decision-making, they find themselves continually tied up in knots and unable to take purposeful action.

In an earlier chapter we touched on how consciousness and intelligence can get in the way of riches. Too much questioning and thinking slows you down. With the advent of the New Age Movement, Far Eastern influence and consciousness-raising groups, we have been lifted to higher levels of awareness and understanding about ourselves and our relation to the universe. Notwithstanding the progress made here, undue reflection about the ramifications of every act will throw you into the standstill of inertia. We are all familiar with Descartes' proclamation, "I think, therefore, I am". This has been rephrased by Western pragmatists to "I act, therefore I am." Ram Dass, the intuitive business philosopher has observed, "I am, therefore, thinking is *one of the things that I do...* along with sensing, playing and taking action." Successful entrepreneurs live by such axioms as "Give me a person of action, not a thinker." Socrates said, "He who would move the world must first move himself." If you would move mountains, you must first move yourself.

The plain truth is, the more information and knowledge you have and the more expanded your consciousness, the greater are your options and potential anxiety. That is, as your imagination, vision and powers of mind increase, you have more degrees of personal freedom and choice. And as the number of choices multiply, so does your uncertainty and anxiety, *unless* you have mastered the art of dealing with this phenomenon so that action follows thought effortlessly and consistently.

Keep in mind that *energy follows thought, then action.* A shortcut, easy way out of this option-overload dilemma is to reduce your informational intake and avoid any reflections on life's great questions. Forget about any moral justification for your activities. Go all out for the buck. Channel your imagination and time strictly toward a product or service that meets a need in society, regardless of how ignoble that need might be. For example, you might get involved in the production and marketing of more violent film and television scripts, or enter into a business that perpetuates the existence of drunken drivers on the highways.

We can all look around us and see those who, judging from appearances at least, act without scruples, catering to the baser needs of others with little regard for any damaging consequences, yet seem to be raking in big money. This is a route you can pursue. Since taking action is such a crucial component of achieving success, one way to go about it is by negating your consciousness and knocking out all those tough decision points at one blow. Instead of wrestling with any moral issues or value nuisances of the mind, put your sights smack on whatever out there is bringing in the gravy. This coupled with a single-minded purpose and desire for making barrels of dollars will propel you from rags to riches as surely as the sun goes down each day.

If you are a person of high integrity and honesty, struggling to act in accordance with your own sense of what is right, you are probably waiting to hear me say next that any riches and wealth gained at the expense or detriment of others will be temporary, short-lived and above all does not include peace of mind. Only part of this statement is true. Temporary and short-lived? Yes, any actions willfully taken to injure another are going to eventually come back to you in one form or another. No peace of mind? This is a different story. Logic and empirical data would indicate just the opposite. After all, if you have snuffed your awareness and consciousness to the point where you have nil values, ethics or reason for living other than making top dollars, just where are any internal conflicts that would produce uneasiness and guilt to intrude on your peace of mind to be found?

Before you decide to embark on this easy road to riches or start envying those who do, however, fully consider one question: "Why, in all humanness, would you want to if in the process you destroy and retard the truly human lifeblood part of you—your very consciousness?" What kind of price is this to pay? What out there could possibly be important enough to sacrifice this great marvel that has come so far in our evolution, that has the miraculous quality to look upon itself and through the power of creation extend its own self to know and be in ways we have not yet dreamed possible? What greater delight in living than working *with* your conscious awareness rather than acting in ways that denigrate, dismiss and destroy it?

There are other arguments that could be advanced for not just going merrily on your way to the buck and letting the immoral chips fall where they may. Rather than belabor this issue, let's move on with those insights and guidelines that will help you pick up the pace in gaining financial prosperity while at the same time nourishing your inner conscious wealth. The two needn't be at arms if you go about it correctly.

The secret lies in learning how to establish an action ideology whereby you are able to unravel your goals, priorities and values to act quickly and creatively under all circumstances. Your aim is to build up to a high momentum action flow that is immune to demands and distractions which get you sidetracked. In our new leisure era with increased personal freedom, this is one of humanity's most perplexing undertakings. You get started on one path of action, then along comes another demand or desire that you find yourself drawn into, holding up progress on the first. This results in a futile chain of behaviors where you find yourself zigzagging back and forth, off course, losing months, perhaps years of time before you ever consummate your mission and discover the financial independence awaiting you.

Let's say you have come up with a new idea for a catering business and plan to start drawing up a proposal tonight after your part-time job. A dozen things can happen to vie for your attention. Just as you get your outline all spread out, you receive a telephone call from a close relative who has become ill and needs a ride to the hospital. A special sweetheart stops by unexpectedly and invites you out to one of your favorite restaurants. Your daughter has a bad day at school and needs to talk about it. Dishes are in the sink and need to be done. A nostalgic tune on the radio evokes memories of a sad period in your life and your mind wanders.

At every step of the way toward financial gains there will be an influx of events and people competing for your time. Some situations are more readily circumvented and corrected than others. Your aim is to stay on course and still remain in good conscience about what you are doing. Once you are fully clear about your objectives, values and priorities, even the most difficult decisions become easier. Take the five situations just mentioned. What can you do and still be in good conscience? A number of solutions are available.

Situation No. 1: In the case of a sick relative who needs attention, you make a quick telephone call to a trustworthy friend to take her to the hospital. If no one is available, reassure her that everything is going to be all right, then put her in a taxi at your expense. You visit her at the hospital later. If your relative's condition is too serious, go with her and bring your work along. While she's seeing the doctor, you can continue your project.

When someone close to you is in pain or unhappy, it is natural to want to help them and take away their grief. This is good. What also happens when we empathize with another's bad fortune, is that a flood of emotions captures our consciousness and can prevent us from thinking and acting effectively if we let it. This is not so good. We say to ourselves, "How can I possibly finish this report when my dear friend, Betty, is lying in the hospital and about to have an operation? I'm too worried and upset to think about anything else." The truth is, giving your full attention to the work at hand is the best thing you can be doing under these circumstances. Sitting idly, fretting and worrying will do absolutely nothing to help your friend in the operating room. This isn't callous or unfeeling. It's a healthy, re-channeling of your energy. Some of the warmest, most loving and caring persons I know have managed to work productively during sad and stressful periods. You can do the same.

Situation No. 2: Your sweetheart has tempted you with dinner at your favorite restaurant. Give him a terrific hug for being so thoughtful and tell him you'll take a raincheck for Friday night when you're free. You not only have something to look forward to, but will be blessed with the good feelings and strength of mind that result from asserting yourself and staying with your decision. And next time a temptation comes your way it will be even easier.

Situation No. 3: Your daughter has a problem she wants to discuss. Let her take a few minutes to get things off her chest and feel better, then give her your support and tell her you'd like to talk longer about it after you finish work on your project and have more time to spend. If you are a mother or father who is working at home with young children, you need to carefully consider which hours you plan to allocate for being with your family and what time is to be devoted to your work. Don't expect to be a superwoman or superman and do two full time jobs concurrently. This will only leave you feeling frazzled and frustrated. Get some outside help with the children and household chores or find an office away from home to do your work. Many offices are available to share at little or no cost. University classrooms and library facilities can provide the quiet and solitude for working on your projects until your budget permits a private office.

Situation No. 4: A minor chore like dirty dishes in the sink will never intrude on your mind if you are serious about entrepreneurship and are following the guidelines in this book. Build the habit of consciously dismissing any miscellaneous tasks and distractions that threaten your time. Remember, you want to plan your day around the important functions in your life, not around household chores like doing the dishes or cleaning out the closets.

Situation No. 5: Keeping nostalgic music from reaching your ears is easily under your control. This can be prevented by working in a different place, keeping the radio off or wearing earplugs. Everything around you has some influence over your state of mind and productivity. In the next chapter you'll learn some specific procedures for how to set up your environment to support your goals.

The crucial factor in all of your decisions is your constancy of purpose and dedication to the entrepreneurial work you have set out to accomplish. Your relatives, sweethearts and children would probably never have considered calling on you to attend to their needs while you were at your nine-to-five job. Except in cases of true emergency, the same policy should be made clear to them now. *Your* work is important. In all likelihood, it is far more important than what you were doing for someone else for a paycheck. It is your responsibility to settle this with yourself and others so that you are not continually caught up in nagging feelings of guilt and conflict every time a demand is made on your time and a tough decision needs to be made. If most of us did half as much in our own interests and with regard to our personal value systems as we have done for our teachers and employers over the years, our lives, and world, would undoubtedly be better.

Let us turn now to some thornier issues.

Resolving New Age Conflicts

Today's entrepreneur faces problems unique to our modern age. As we move into a different style of living, thinking and being, a whole new range of challenges and conflicts stands before us. During the long era of the work ethic when we were caught up in a work-for-survival and work-for-salvation mode, there was little freedom of mind to consider the many prosperity options or individual morality choices. The bulk of our waking hours were spent eeking out a living: we neither had the time nor the awareness to think much beyond our basic needs of food, shelter, health and simple pleasures. The contradictions and dilemmas we are facing today rarely presented themselves.

In the pages that follow we examine some of the recent phenomena springing forth from leaving the work ethic behind and moving into a leisure and entrepreneurial epoch. As you go forward, keep in mind that every thought you have and choice you make is wrought between polarities. One of the hurdles to success is finding your domain within each polarity so as to act naturally and swiftly without vacillation or becoming deadlocked.

To reiterate: one of the greatest deterrents to riches is having unresolved issues and conflicts clanking around in your head keeping you from taking decisive action. Until these time-thugs have been sought out and dealt with, they will forever be scurrying about pulling you off course. Only when you are able to declare a moratorium on these inner rumblings can you be released from the paralysis of procrastination.

Three modern day dichotomies we face are: (1)Material prosperity vs. spiritual fulfillment; (2)Goal-oriented future-living vs. living in the present; and (3)Predictability vs uncertainty. Let's look at each of these.

Material prosperity vs. spiritual fulfillment

In Chapter Two you were introduced to the need for having a substantial amount of money. It was hinted at how this could be a foundation for spiritual wealth as well. The quest today is for a perspective comprehensive enough to contain the rewards of financial independence without throwing away the spiritual enrichment and consciousness expansion many of us have gained over the past decade. In talking with would-be entrepreneurs, I find that there is still a basic conflict running rampant, an uneasiness about the inherent right to material prosperity and all it holds for us.

On the one hand, we pay lip service to feeling comfortable with personal wealth, seeming to have no apparent contradiction, while at the same time, never quite coming to terms with it in our guts. This is reflected in both the ways in which we spend money and our attitudes toward the acquisition of our adult toys. For example, many of us must justify the functional utility of a product before we feel comfortable about buying it. We sell ourselves on spending a bunch of money on a luxury car by emphasizing its safety features and low maintenance. We talk about how we will be able to balance our budget with our new personal computer when all we really want is to play games with it. We tell our children that our new 14-Karat gold Rolex watch will last forever, and convince ourselves of its investment value.

Granted such self-justifications are not always the case or true for everyone. Mostly, we find ourselves making apologies and defending our purchases when we are around those who are lower on the financial totem pole. A tinge of guilt is especially likely to tug at you if you have a widowed mother, close friend or sister in need when you make an extravagant, impulsive purchase. To a large extent this has to do with the leftover remnants of the Calvin work ethic invading our thinking; we aren't quite sure we deserve great wealth and the goodies of life, or that we dare enjoy ourselves completely.

What you want to assess are the factors coloring your emotions in these instances. Ask yourself, "What does being a responsible consumer mean to me?" When you make lavish purchases for yourself and others around you lack, is this truly money you believe should have been spent on them? To what extent are you responsible for others' financial welfare? And which others? Your immediate family: mother, father, children? Your extended family: aunts and uncles, nephews and nieces? Your community and the world at large: the homeless, aged, diseased? This is not a call to be callous and think only of yourself, just the opposite. What I would like you to do is clarify your consumer value system by pondering where you believe your responsibility lies in these matters.

One way to do this is by reaching a definite decision point concerning the percentage of your income and profits you wish to allot to others. This allotment might be in the form of gifts such as we give at Christmas, birthdays and other special occasions. Keep in mind also that many times a thoughtful and more cherished gift can cost much less than one bought in haste with little forethought about the person's wants.

If you give to a foundation, church or special fund, again think in terms of what allotment is appropriate with respect to your value system. For example, if you have a special concern for the well-being of the homeless, you may wish to allot more monetary support for this cause. Many families have made the decision at Christmas time to forego the usual trinket giving to each other and use the money instead to assist a cause in which they believe. Being a responsible consumer and remaining guilt-free means taking the time to think through your expenditures.

Time Block No. 13
Material Prosperity

Tonight between 5:30 and 6:30 p.m. write out a one sentence response to each of the five questions below. If this time is impossible, decide on another time *now* and write it down in the space provided below:

"I, ___________________________________(your name), am taking steps to become financially responsible between the hours of_________on_________(day of week).

Questions to respond to:

1. Do you sometimes give donations or gifts because of what others will think instead of what you prefer to do? Why?

2. Do you spend more money on some people than you would like to? Who?

3. Do you spend less money on others than you would like? Who?

4. Do you believe that you do not deserve to have more material goods than members of your family? Your close friends? Others? Who?

5. Do you feel that you do not deserve to have expensive items unless everyone in the world has the same?

These appraisals will assist you in bringing into the open your beliefs about spending money and material goods ownership. The further you go in clearing up any below-the-surface conflicts you have about the acquisition of material goods, the less energy fixation and energy depletion you are going to have in this connection. Your objective is to reach a decision about your consumer habits, and shift your behavior in that direction. Here are some guidelines:

(A)Observe, acknowledge and accept your current spending habits. This is a necessary base from which change and improvement can occur. Avoid getting into a dialogue with yourself and rationalizing or justifying previous expenditures.
(B)Forgive yourself for past impulsive buying that you are now regretting.
(C)Give yourself permission to be rich and prosperous.
(D)Set up some purchase-reward contingencies for yourself. For example, after you have mastered four consecutive weeks of twelve or more time block hours toward your objectives, buy yourself something you have been wanting. It could be something useful or something frivolous. Decide how much you want to spend *beforehand*. Your purchase might be an item as simple as a bouquet of flowers, a bottle of cologne or a new book. Or it could be a major purchase like an outfit of clothes, a luggage set or a fine piece of furniture.

A survey of successful entrepreneurs has shown that they habitually make a conscious choice to reward themselves upon the completion of a project or important phase of work. A highly successful real estate agent I know takes herself on a fun shopping spree with a specified amount of dollars after every close of escrow. A mainframe computer representative loves taking his wife and children out for a special dinner after a big contract is cinched. Some successful authors I'm acquainted with love to treat themselves to things like new bookcases, file cabinets and different software aids upon completion of a manuscript.

As you become more involved in your entrepreneurial affairs, you'll probably find your consumer interests shifting to those products related to your lifework. An entrepreneur who started out doing wallpapering in residential homes told me his earliest dream was to have one of the fancy fold-up wallpaper tables that are used to cut out wallpaper. With his first big job, this was his reward to himself. Whether your expenditures are for practical items or just something you want in order to satisfy a whim matters little. It is your conscious choice about what you are doing that makes a difference. When you make a conscious choice about your purchases, your energy will no longer be tied up with guilt and regrets. An exhilaration and buoyancy will take over in its place. Whenever you are true to your choices you'll find yourself the recipient of this marvelous feeling state. And as you become more in command and the creator in your life, this happy state of mind will be a predominant force.

Time-Use Misgivings

Having misgivings about the things we spend money on and how much we are spending is just one source of frustration for most people. Another form of conflict related to the acquisition of riches that we fall prey to is the amount of time put in toward this end rather than for more "worthwhile" endeavors. For instance, as the hours required on your entrepreneurial projects increase, you may start to worry about the little time you have available for your loved ones, feel that you are neglecting community responsibilities or missing the boat in your spiritual development. Mind tricks we have traditionally used to assuage this time-use remorse are: "With the extra dollars, I can give my family and friends more of the material things they deserve." "Later, I will devote more time to Little League and attend personal enrichment seminars." Other arguments we pose to ourselves say: "I will give money to charities instead of my service." "I will only devote my time to entrepreneurial enterprises for a few years, amass a fortune, then I'll be able to retire and make up for all the areas of my life that have been neglected."

Rationalizations such as these mostly miss the mark. The fact that we even need to indulge in this kind of mind deception is suggestive of the problems inherent from such a position. Until the conflict is brought to the surface and consciously resolved, it is going to widdle away at your creative energy. In an earlier chapter you were given a Time Block exercise to assist you in putting the important dimensions of your life together harmoniously for conflict-free living. Take a moment now to examine your own attitudes with respect to money and time usage.

The greatest struggle I've found frequently lies with the new age dreamer and visionary who has reached a high plane of cognitive integration and awareness, nonetheless is forever living on the border of abject material poverty as compared with his or her less sensitive entrepreneurial brothers and sisters. Rejecting what is perceived as "the business world" and the playing of money games, this type person has turned her attention inward to explore the vast subjective terrain, without ever coming to grips with her own creative action force as it could impact on the world to give both herself and society a commodity of value.

Only when you become crystal clear about your right to riches in relation to how your time is divided will you be free from disruptive doubts and have the level of power to move with precision toward prosperity goals. Emerson has remarked in one of his essays, "Man (and woman) was born to be rich". Understand that you have a natural, unequivocal right to the riches of the universe, and this includes more than fresh air to breathe and clean water to drink. Money has never been the root of all evil; lack of money is. A poverty consciousness will slam the door to riches faster than anything. Nor do you need to suffer through some arduous struggle before you are entitled to that prosperity. Dealing with the problems stemming from a poverty lifestyle is much more demanding and disagreeable than just going ahead and making the choice to take those crucial steps up to riches. As someone has observed, "Money talks, but poverty just pinches."

Your Self-Image & Wealth

The self-image and belief system you hold has a major bearing on the events in your life and the amount of wealth destined to be yours. Far too many people are unable to conceive of themselves having abundance. A close friend, Greg, brought this home to me recently. He'd had a string of bad luck and taken a beating financially. Greg had done me a number of favors on different occasions and I wanted to give him something special and cheer him up. As I was walking past an art gallery in Carmel, California, I spotted this marvelous miniature Rolls Royce. It was even red, his favorite color. While it wasn't an auto you get into and drive off, I was sure he'd appreciate it. And it fit my value system perfectly on cars: no gasoline to buy, no insurance premiums to pay, no maintenance, and Greg would never have to worry about it crashing in transit. Or so I thought. I paid the clerk at the art gallery the hefty tab and beaming happily with my purchase, hand-delivered it to Greg.

His eyes first lit up, then pausing he said, "It's too expensive. I can't accept that," though he knew full well that I could afford it. Finally, he reluctantly took the gift, but it was obvious he didn't feel comfortable owning such a lavish object. A few months later when he moved to a new location, the Rolls Royce was wrapped and sent through the mail. Not surprisingly, the exquisite auto arrived at its destination broken in a hundred pieces. Just a coincidence? I doubt it. Greg could never quite see himself as the owner of such an expensive gift and as a result it vanished from his life. With Greg's poverty self-image, anything of material value that came into his life was destined to get lost, be stolen or crumble in one way or another.

You will find too, that items of monetary value and wealth cannot come into your world and stay there unless the images you hold of yourself support them. We have all heard the riches-to-rags true stories of those people who have inherited or been given a sizable amount of money only to find themselves penniless a short time later. If you hold fast to images of lack and poverty, that is exactly what is going to appear at your doorstep.

One of my clients who has not yet gotten over his poverty-minded hump manages to jeopardize every money-making opportunity that presents itself. Although he inherited a sizable amount of cash, Bill was never able to incorporate this into his self-image. He persisted in seeing himself without any money. First, he kept the inherited funds tied up in long term, low interest bearing notes in a savings account, unable to trust himself with it. Although on several occasions, Bill was offered high-return, low-risk investment opportunities, he always wavered. He couldn't get a picture of himself as a successful money-maker. Sadly, this indigent consciousness took over in his life. He lost his job and in three short months totally went through the entire sum of his inheritance, without so much as ever applying any portion of it to a business enterprise or sound investment. All around us we see the Gregs and Bills whose nickel-and-dime self images are keeping them from financial independence.

Conversely, and on the brighter side, whatever you are able to create in your mind and continue to envision as part of your world will more than likely come about. Regardless of how much you might presently be in debt or lacking in those things you desire, when you release yourself from this unacceptable context and replace your internal images with those things you do want, soon the external manifestations will find a place in your life. Start reinforcing a prosperity self-image by doing the following exercise.

Time Block No. 14
Instilling a Wealth Consciousness

Set aside five minutes each morning after breakfast to dwell on the statements given below. Repeat them out loud and commit them to memory so that they become a part of your daily self-talk.

(1)I have an inherent right to the riches of this world.
(2)I feel, look and act prosperous.
(3)I see myself as a person of wealth.
(4)Money is good.
(5)Money is flowing into my life as I fulfill my creative mission.

Goal-oriented future-living vs. living in the present

Another dilemma of our leisure epoch that confronts and confuses us is how we can live within the present moment, reaping the rewards of the here and now while simultaneously entering into goal behaviors directed toward future payoffs. This conflict is relatively new to Western Civilization and has come to us from greater exposure to Far Eastern thought and an increasing acceptance of the validity of many of their insights, albeit being as yet unable to fully integrate these into our Western models.

A dominant characteristic of homo sapiens is our teleological nature, setting up goals throughout the lifespan and structuring our time toward their culmination. The conflict we face is how these future-oriented behaviors can be rectified with present activities so that we are not always "living for the future" and missing something vital within the present. How do you keep a moment-by-moment presence of mind as you go about your daily affairs? Eastern philosophers refer to this as a state of "timelessness", a mode of being where you are able to so completely lose yourself in the present that there is no thought or fear of future events. Nor do past mistakes, misgivings or other emotionally-laden thoughts from previous conditioning interfere with your current state of mind. Your thoughts neither ramble about in the refuge of past painful experiences and regrets nor meander off toward future outcome worries and uncertainties. As a result, you are "free" in the purist sense of the word, free to act spontaneously and creatively, giving your full attention and best to where you are and what you are doing right now.

Eastern philosophers maintain that until we are able to totally release ourselves from these past-future thought invaders, we are destined to be discontented and dissatisfied with our present lot (see especially the writings of Krishnamurti). For even as we touch those pinnacles of success for which we have been striving, the glow of our achievement fades quickly. Boredom and depression arrive and the forces of self-destruction set in. To counter this trend, another goal is set up for some distant future. Thus, we find ourselves forever entrenched in an endless cycle of future-living, always anticipating that our lot will get better, and never quite grasping the perfection of the moment. On the other hand, if no goal or challenge is set before us, we are likely to become too comfortable and wallow in excesses: eating, drinking and sleeping too much. Or we find various ways to distract ourselves. Neither route is desirable or necessary.

In actuality, there need be no conflict and contradiction in present-living versus goal-oriented living. The imposition lies more with our current language limitations and difficulty in shaking our consciousness free from these constraints. For it is by initially establishing your clarity of purpose, setting goals and having a plan-of-action that opens the door to complete presence of mind and spontaneity. A plan-of-action is not meant to be a rigid, carved-out-of-cement structure but a dynamic, flexible system which is there for your convenience to keep you on target and give you the automatic selectivity-mindedness so important for moving swiftly and effortlessly and with streamline focus.

It is this well-thought-out, charted course of action that allows you the freedom to be in the present moment without worry or undue concern for future outcomes. Failure to lay out viable lifetime goals and subgoals along with a plan for their realization so that you stay on course is just the thing that will throw you out of the present and into those past-future thought-pits of futility, fear and frustration that Eastern philosophers warn against.

And it is precisely this distinguishing teleological characteristic of man and woman that permits the playful, creative spirit of the present moment out of which we are continuously in touch with the cosmos and our raison d'etre. Within these time boundaries of purpose and passion for those goals you are committed to, your spirit is released and can romp about to do its best for you.

How do you shift into such a mode of being and stay there? The Time Block exercise below will help you master this remarkable state.

Time Block No. 15
"Timelessness"

Take three minutes each day before plunging into your Personal Play Project to consciously remind, direct and encourage yourself as follows:

(1)Keep a clear perspective.
(2)Concentrate fully on the task at hand.
(3)*Decide* to not let past-future rattlings capture your consciousness. When these thoughts enter your mind, gently let them pass on through. Pay them no heed and they will have no hold on you.
(4)Stick with each PPP to its completion, unless there are legitimate extenuating circumstances.
(5)Trust in yourself and the universe.

Predictability vs. uncertainty

All of us need a "loop of predictability" in the vital areas of our life. That is, we need to know what consequences to expect (from ourselves, others and our environment) based on the actions we take, thoughts we think and feelings we project.

For example, you may know that expressing sexual overtures toward your sweetheart elicits similar feelings in him or her; that every Sunday morning like clockwork your mother telephones; and that whenever you enter the freeway, it is jammed with traffic. Whether the events in your life are favorable or unfavorable, desirable or undesirable, you feel relatively secure in your ability to accurately foretell what is about to happen.

If, instead of the usual, your mate's response to loving overtures suddenly turned to anger, the telephone calls from your mother on Sunday abruptly ceased, and you got on the freeway one morning and found no other cars, your tension level and blood pressure would likely rise substantially. And if your expectations were constantly jolted in this fashion in too many areas of your life, you would wind up at a mental institution in short order. That is indeed exactly what "going crazy" is: not being able to predict and make sense of what's happening, either for yourself or in your surroundings. We can never completely predict what a totally aberrant personality is going to do because even he does not know.

A measure of predictability then keeps our lives in balance and we build up a pattern of actions that flow automatically and easily. We feel secure, not necessarily happy or worthy, but nevertheless comfortable and sane. It is the same reason why many of us stay in a bad situation: a marriage that isn't working, an abusive relationship or an objectionable job. Being able to predict what is going to happen, regardless of how unpalatable it might be, is apparently better than venturing out into the unknown.

It is when you step outside of the regular routine or in some way move outside of your present loop of predictability and state of comfortable equilibrium that uncertainty and tension result. This could occur when you take a vacation to an unfamiliar area, purchase your first home, seek a new sexual companion or other novel situations. You experience the stress of both choice and outcome uncertainty.

When you disturb your equilibrium by generating changes in your lifestyle and surrounding environment, although you open up new options, your world becomes less predictable and there is temporarily more uncertainty to handle. Simultaneously, as your time space of options increases with choices leading you to new goals and horizons, your range of predictability expands. A larger vision with greater possibilities becomes evident. With more pieces of life's puzzle settling into place, you can see farther and more lucidly. The scope of your world swells. The mysteries of the universe unravel before your eyes and you marvel at what lies before you. Anticipation and excitement fill the air.

The more you can extend this predictability loop so that your cognitions, sentiments and actions unfold in a way that is consistent with your overall purpose and the expression of your unique personality, the greater you pronounce your sense of self-worth and well-being. As you go about your daily activities, you bask in a glow that all is right with the world. Everything you do magically turns out perfect. Old boundaries fall away to be replaced by new freedoms and prosperity.

Always, however, as you reach out to new ways of living and introducing innovative behaviors, products and services to your environment, you will experience an uncertainty gap. And the more your consciousness and world is expanded through the creative act, the more disruption to your equilibrium. The ideal state turns out to be then neither one of equilibrium nor certainty.

Yet, since the days of Newtonian physics, painting the world as a giant machine of cause-effect chains, absolute laws and basic denominations, we have quested for shreds of certainty. Ah, but to know just one thing...definitely, permanently, eternally. Even as Heisenberg's Uncertainty Principle has burst on the scene exploding our false sense of security with its final certitude that "there is no certainty", we cling to "the predictables" in our lives, unable to break loose, go out on a limb and venture into unknown realms where we might discover the many heretofore mysterious riches and luxuries of the universe.

The fact of the matter is: *we do not need certainty in our lives.* Furthermore, we do not even *want* total predictability and certainty. For with complete predictability lies the end of new forms and creations and mind expansion. With a closed circuit of cause-effect links, we sacrifice our gift of choice and free will. What we need instead are only the means to deal effectively as we stand before new decision points, challenges and opportunities. What we require today is the insight and trust to act correctly and confidently even in the face of outcome uncertainty.

Uncertainty & the risk factor

This leads us to the risk factor surrounding decision-making, another key variable affecting your success. Many of us mentally anguish over every choice in our path. We worry about falling on our faces. We fret over the consequences to our family if we make a wrong move and fail. We tremble at the thought of losing what we have.

If you have such fears, what can you do about them? First of all, know that the best of entrepreneurs do occasionally take a dive. No matter how much you prepare yourself, you can expect to make mistakes, small ones for sure and possibly some colossal ones. But it is not a lack of mistakes that distinguish the successful from the unsuccessful; it is how they are dealt with when they occur. The giants of entrepreneurship will be challenged and stimulated by problems and setbacks that arise. Those doomed to failure will be devastated by them. It is what you do when you strike out that makes the difference. Just because you fall into a puddle doesn't mean you need to lie down in it. Remember, he who never climbed, never failed.

Given the right mind state and potent time use, a loss of $5,000 or even $5,000,000 simply won't matter in the final analysis because you have the capabilities to turn every disaster around into an even better opportunity. As you look into the jaws of uncertainty, trust yourself and the universe. Learn to acknowledge your fears and take a positive stand against them. It is all right to be fearful. It is not all right to let your fears prevent you from taking decisive, effective action.

Time Block No. 16
Risk-Taking

Whenever you are confronted with a troublesome decision that involves a measure of risk, repeat the following affirmation to yourself.

"I, ______________________________________(your name) know that the only real risk in life is to take no risks. After preparing myself as best I know how, I always act swiftly and confidently."

Attitude Shifts & Action Steps
On-Going Time Blocks

Time Block No. 14
Instilling a Wealth Consciousness

Take two minutes each morning after breakfast to repeat the five affirmations provided in this exercise.

Time Block No. 15
"Timelessness"

Each day before beginning your PPP, spend three minutes according to the instructions for this exercise.

Time Block No. 16
Risk-Taking

Whenever you are confronted with a decision involving risk, repeat the affirmation given.

1V
Enjoying your Success & Prosperity

"Only a person who can live with himself (or herself) can enjoy the gift of leisure."
—Henry Greber

8
Staying Fused With A Playful, Creative Spirit

"A strong passion for any object will ensure success, for the desire of the end will point out the means."

—WILLIAM HAZLITT

Building Desire Blocks

Having a burning desire to put your ideas into action is the single most important factor for your success as an entrepreneur. Becoming involved in entrepreneurial projects that align with your personality, needs and values, without being unduly concerned over market trends, will go a long way toward kindling your desire and sustaining your interest when problems arise. Having a strong, built-in desire reserve leads you to a successful plan-of-action, gets you through the necessary hours of love-labor, and carries you over, around, under or through any obstacles that get in the way. It stands to reason then that employing every means possible to catalyze this desire and keep you at peak creative performance will strengthen your personal fortune.

The five guidelines and time blocks in this chapter are designed to give you the necessary impetus to stay pivoted toward success regardless of your current situation, unproductive past habit patterns, or future events that may threaten your goals.

Guideline 1.
Act Promptly

You should already have taken preliminary action-steps toward achieving your Personal Play Project. A reminder: You will never be 100% ready to begin anything. Some doubts and insecurities are always going to creep into your consciousness. "Can I do it?" "Am I capable? What if I fail?" "There is so much I need to know." "Maybe I should think about this awhile." This kind of self-talk and action-stopper is typical before a new undertaking. Nevertheless, if you have laid the foundation by following the recommendations suggested throughout this book, are making the attitude shifts and have completed the exercises to select your PPP, you are more than ready to act.

Start following through immediately with your ideas and prosperity program even though you do not have every detail worked out. You want to become engaged and establish an action-pattern while your enthusiasm is on the upswing. You can correct for errors and re-assess as you go, but it is mandatory that you cease vacillating about whether you should or could be doing something else. Give your full attention and commitment to the project at hand. If your PPP requires modifications, you can make these changes as you progress. The knowledge and skills required for the success of your project will be evident as you become more involved. Then you can selectively learn everything that is necessary.

You'll find this to be a tremendous time-saver over traditional approaches. When you have a definite purpose in mind you are able to cut through a lot of extraneous information, see more clearly what is and what is not relevant to your goals and short circuit dead end routes that get you off course and waste time. For example, it has been demonstrated that students who enter an educational program with notions about what they want beforehand are able to extract the appropriate information much easier and quicker than those who have no personal objectives to which they're relating the material. Similarly, it has been found that when you try to figure something out for yourself before you are instructed or told what to do, you are more likely to retain the information and put it to use.

By staying alert and following the procedures in this book, it will soon be obvious if you are off target and at that time you can make the necessary adjustments and changes. Even when you are on the wrong track, it is in the process of doing that your creativity unfolds and points the way to your next move.

Many of our greatest inventions were discovered by serendipity. That is, the most brilliant minds in history have been dead wrong in their approach and analysis of what would be the best solution to the problem at hand, and only by accident did they discover the magic ingredient or link. Nonetheless, it would never have been discovered had they not been taking action toward a particular goal. Sitting around waiting for the gods to wave a banner of certitude over your head before you get started will not only jeopardize your fortune-to-be but is likely to give you a throbbing headache and throw you into depression.

Guideline 2.
Forget Obstacles & Focus On Results

Practically any self-improvement book you pick up on achieving success will advise readers to list the obstacles standing between them and their desired results. This is also found in the educational setting. High school and college instructors encourage students in problem-solving disciplines to cast about for obstacles and how they can be eliminated. Indeed, a problem is typically defined as having an obstacle lodged between you and the solution. And in certain professions, notably law, there is almost a religious fervor for digging out hidden problems and obstacles for every kind of situation. (If none are immediately apparent, you can be sure an enterprising attorney will find some!) Opportunities are constantly overlooked and missed by our undue attention to these emotionally-laden barricades. Obstacles, problems, hardship and struggle are stone-carved into our work ethic society.

The rationale behind this sort of obstacle-thinking sounds logical enough. It is argued that we cannot fight ghosts or unknowns and therefore need to be aware of anything that might interfere with our objectives. My experience in dealing with entrepreneurs and talking with prosperous people, however, is that most of us would never have even gotten started if we were aware of all the problems that might arise. Or if you did have the courage to jump in and take the risk, you would feel weighted down instead of having the excited anticipation that is the lifeblood of success. It is the one reason why we probably have not fully evolved a sixth sense to look totally into the future and predict events. The mass of obstacles stacked against us could be overpowering.

"But", you protest, "Shouldn't I know what I'm letting myself in for beforehand?" Actually, no. It is not the obstacles that make a difference to your riches. You achieve prosperity according to your spirit of purpose, direction, creative expression and how well you are structuring your time. Obstacles have nothing to do with it. Nor do you want to give your attention and energy to those things you don't wish to happen.

If you acquire the habit of acting within each moment, adamantly directed toward the results you seek, you will find that you have the inner resources to manage whatever comes up. With this approach you take things in stride rather than subjecting yourself to the squelching effect of having everything negative dumped on you all at once, before you even get started. Remember, "Obstacles are what you see when you take your eyes off the goal".

Rather than concerning yourself with all the logical reasons why something cannot be done and cluttering up your mind with discouragement, keep your attention centered on your PPP and the results you expect. Make your list not of obstacles but of the rewards you will gain. To do this, stop for a moment now and do the exercise below.

Time Block No. 17
"Millionaire Play Sheet" Update

In the beginning of the book you were asked to draft your **Millionaire Play Sheet**, brainstorming about all the benefits that money would bring into your life. Now that you have had a chance to crystalize your creative enterprise and ambitions further, I want you to update your ideas and get more specific. Take four minutes and list all the riches and by-products of riches you are going to experience upon achieving your PPP objectives. They may be intangible rewards such as greater peace of mind, love and fame. Or they might be the tangible, material rewards of a summer cottage on the oceanfront, a yacht, ski gear and a trip to the mountains.

After you have exhausted your list, take a magic marker with your favorite color and underline those rewards that stir your emotions. Then put the list on a wall in front of your bed so that it is the first thing you see every morning when you awaken. It is helpful to also pin up pictures that represent your desires. For example, it could be a sailboat, a word processor or a piece of furniture, whatever you fancy. Some of your pictures may need to be symbolic: a quiet meadow for peace of mind, a majestic mountain scene for spiritual fulfillment and so on. In the next few days, thumb through magazines and cut out those pictures appropriate to your objectives.

As you continue to formulate your plans and structure your time in balance with your priorities, keep in mind that the progress you are making toward your goals is sometimes obscured. At different times you will feel like you are losing ground, are stagnant, and failing to advance as rapidly as you hoped. Although you need to constantly be alert and flexible to innovative ways to reach your goals, often we become disheartened and give up just short of success. Remind yourself at these crisis points that insofar as you have chosen a PPP worthy of your creative talents and are consistently structuring your time to support this endeavor, you needn't have any doubts about attracting success. You have within you everything you need to rise up to your fondest hopes and dreams.

Whenever you undergo the slightest hint of doubt or dismay, get in the habit of instantly turning your attention to your **Millionaire Play Sheet** of desired outcomes. Emotionalize these until your appetite is fairly craving their culmination, until every fiber and cell of your body feels their existence. If the rewards on your list are not sustaining your interest as well as they might, go back and play around with your wants and desires in relation to your PPP and see what changes you can make.

Guideline 3.
Insure Prosperity With "External Props"

You want to set up your external environment in such a way that it becomes easier and easier to follow through on your prosperity projects. In reordering your day toward entrepreneurial goals, you are substituting new activities that initially require more energy than doing things the old way. This is because the new behaviors haven't yet become an automatic, regular part of your life. You are still going through decision points and pauses of uncertainty for each change. The smoother this transition period can be made until the success habits have been firmly established and routine (done seemingly without thinking), the less fatigue you will experience. And the more zest and vigor you'll have available.

Therefore, it is smart to set up your environment (your home, office, or wherever you are spending the most time in carrying out your PPP) so that it requires more effort to go back to the old ways than to follow through on your new commitments.

Take a close look at these surroundings in conjunction with your previous pattern of time use. Let's say you have blocked out the hours between 7:00 p.m and 9:00 p.m. to make telephone calls and do research on your seminar project survey. You have decided that this is the best time to call because people are more likely to be home during the dinner hour. However, this was the time during which you usually had dinner and watched television. So far, there has been no problem with your motivation. You're fired up about your new plans and are making your telephone calls right on schedule. You haven't turned the television set on once. But only four days have passed since you began.

Right now, before any trace of doubt or discouragement occurs (and they sneak up on you at the least expected times), you want to prepare yourself against a former habit lapse. Therefore, unplug the television set, wrap the cord around it, then take a piece of string and tie several knots at the end of the wire.

To revert to your former behavior will require you to (1)find the scissors and cut the string; (2)uncoil the cord and (3)plug it back in the wall socket. If your television watching behavior is entrenched, you may need to cart the set down to the basement, lock it in a closet and put the key in an inconvenient place, or even loan it to a friend for awhile. That is for you to determine.

Perhaps another habit is reading romance novels an hour or so before dropping off to sleep at night. For the time being you have lost interest in them and are spending this period engaged in activities related to your PPP. Again, you want to rearrange your exterior environment to make it as inconvenient as possible to go back to the old ways. Box up the novels you have on hand and store them away.

Look around you and rid yourself of any temptations that might act to pull you off course. I am not suggesting that you deny yourself all those former activities which gave you pleasure. These can be scheduled in your recreation hours. As you stay with your PPP and it becomes more and more rewarding, you'll find the things you used to enjoy no longer hold much interest for you. They will only be mindless diversions to turn to when you need a break or rest from your first love, your PPP.

Nevertheless, at this early stage in your enterprise you want to make it as easy as possible on yourself to remain on the prosperity path. When you get zapped with an unexpected turn of events (the loan you thought was in the bag falls through; your first seminar bombs; your spouse gets transferred), your old behavior patterns have their arms outstretched, beckoning you back.

The aim then is to check out your new "play space" and rearrange those objects in your environment so that you maximize the effort required to fall into previous nonproductive habits. Obviously, no ploy in itself is going to prevent you from drifting back to old ways. Nevertheless, the cumulative impact definitely makes a difference. Your habits have been with you a long time. You want to use every means possible to prop yourself up until the new prosperity patterns are a regular part of your lifestyle.

Besides rearranging your environment to make the old habits as difficult as possible, the other side of the picture is to give yourself those props which support the new habits. Here is one example of how this is done: To keep your energy level up you have decided to spend a minimum of twenty minutes each morning riding an exercycle. You have an old one down in your basement along with bar bells and other paraphernalia for working out. Although you have had the exercycle over two years you have never been able to motivate yourself to ride it for more than five or ten minutes because, as you have said many times, "It's boring". Actually, it's an invigorating experience. It can even be exciting, enjoyable and a fine learning opportunity.

Begin by bringing the bike upstairs out of the dark basement where you have already been conditioned against the pleasures of riding. Think about your favorite spot in the house or yard. Is it sitting in the living room and looking at the view of the bay (or mountains, trees, city)? Perhaps it's sitting in the back yard listening to the birds sing, the wind rustling through the trees, smelling the scent of the camelias you have just planted. The splendid feature of your exercycle is its versatility. You can position it virtually anywhere, indoors or outdoors and facing in any direction. You can soak up warm sunrays, get a tan, or ride in the cool shade. Best of all, you don't have to worry about traffic.

There are several props you can use to make your cycling more rewarding and insure against boredom. Put on an upbeat music cassette tape. Situate yourself in front of your home video and play back the documentary on investments you recorded three months ago and have not found time to watch. Better yet, put on the cassette you have just received on "How to conduct seminars" (or whatever your business venture is about). Catch up on some telephone calls. Read or dictate letters. You needn't do any of these things, of course. The idea is to combine something you presently enjoy with the cycling until it alone is a source of pleasure.

Start out slowly on the bike, keep track of your mileage and increase the time and wheel-tension as it feels comfortable. If you have scheduled your exercise for early morning, do it before you eat breakfast so you have this to anticipate after finishing. In no time at all, you will be looking forward to getting out of bed and treating yourself to the exercycle. And it will give you extra energy and put many minutes in your day to devote to your business enterprise.

I have intentionally elaborated somewhat at length on the exercycle example, not to pitch you on this particular form of exercise, but to illustrate how you, through opening yourself to a playful, festive mood, can enhance your desire and sell yourself on practically anything you decide to do.

Time Block No. 18
Setting Up External Props

Take fifteen minutes now and play around in your mind with all the new entrepreneurial habits you wish to cultivate. How can you rearrange your physical space to make them easier and more enjoyable? Block times out in your calendar for making these changes.

Guideline 4.
Pick Up The Pace With "Internal Props"

After you have set up your external environment to support your PPP, the next order of business is to reinforce the inner dimensions of your mind for prosperity. Internal props are techniques aimed especially at empowering your subconscious with a stronger desire. As you follow through on your PPP at a conscious level by setting goals, having a plan-of-action, determining priorities and blocking out your time for the new activities, you also need to reach beneath the surface with a program that keeps your subconscious revitalized. This will further dispel any doubt, discontentment and discouragement seeping through to disrupt your progress. You want the new patterns to become reflexive, automatic action, unhindered by any of your conscious mind's rationalizations, excuses and waverings.

Two booster aids that you want to begin using are: **Endless Tape Dynamics** and **Voices of Authority.** Both of these require some preparation. The results will be well worth the time you invest. Follow the instructions given in Time Blocks 19 and 20 below:

Time Block No. 19
Endless Tape Dynamics

The basic tool needed to make use of this technique is a blank audio cassette tape that runs itself through and then keeps repeating nonstop. These are available in short time spans, two to fifteen minutes, depending on their purpose. They have been found effective in language learning, stress reduction, insomnia and for a variety of other objectives. You will be using it as an emotional catalyst and to channel your energies toward your entrepreneurial goals.

You'll first need to purchase one of the blank, five minute, endless tapes from a cassette outlet. After you have the tape, record the script that follows. Repeat the messages until they fill up the entire blank tape. You are now ready to begin. Apply it in two ways: One, along with self-meditation where its messages plug directly into your subconscious, and two, as a repetitive device that repeats its messages regardless of your mental state.

As a repetitive device, listen to the recording anytime during the day or night that is convenient. To use it along with meditation, you want first to put on a self-hypnosis induction tape, then play the endless tape messages that you have recorded. (Self-hypnosis induction tapes can be purchased at New Age book stores.) Employing this technique sends the messages directly into your subconscious where you are more susceptible to suggestion. The dialogue from the script produces a quicker, more lasting effect than when it is played in your normal beta, waking state.

It is recommended that you play the meditation-endless tapes initially for a minimum of two times daily. Mornings when you first awaken and nights, right before dropping off to sleep, produce the best results. Get in the habit of using a cassette alarm clock so that you wake up to the positive prosperity messages rather than the shrill ring of an alarm, nostalgic music or bad news broadcasts from the radio.

Endless Tape Dynamics is one of the most powerful devices discovered for intensifying desire and propelling you toward those rewards you seek. Used consistently, you will have no difficulty in keeping your energy channeled toward the outcomes of your choice.

Endless Tape Dynamics Script

(1)I am thrilled with the PPP I have chosen.

(2)My body tingles with creative energy.

(3)I have enormous energy and enthusiasm for my projects.

(4)I expect success.

(5)I love a good challenge.

(6)I see opportunity everywhere.

(7)I expect a positive outcome in everything I do.

(8)My energy is passionately directed toward my PPP.

(9)I feel myself literally tingling with success.

(10)I have tremendous vitality and stamina.

(11)I thoroughly enjoy what I do.

(12)I have a powerful vision of success.

(13)My projects are stimulating, challenging and fun.

(14)In my mind's eye I can see the completion of my project.

(15)I anticipate success in everything I do.

Note: Feel free to add to this list, keeping in mind that redundancy is good. You want to state your emotions in as many ways as you can to support your goals. Detail your house of emotional desires with as many positive messages as you can dream up.

Time Block No. 20
Voices of Authority

A strong, forceful, authoritarian voice commanding you to feel, think and act in a particular way has been demonstrated to be another powerful determinant of behavior and behavior change. While different persons respond with varying degrees of influence, the **Voice of Authority** is operative for everyone depending on the conditions under which it is given. The basis for this influence is conjectured to stem from our past history and the evolution of consciousness. One notable and brilliant theorist, Julian Jaynes, suggests that before we became truly "conscious" in the sense of making our own decisions, we were governed by inner voices that told us what to do during periods of uncertainty. Over the course of time and as our consciousness evolved, we lost these inner godlike voices and looked outward to external signs, omens, and to our tribe, cultural norms, the legal system, and those in positions of authority to give us direction and tell us what to do under doubtful circumstances.

A number of sociological and psychological experiments indicate that the higher we elevate another to a position of authority, the greater their power and control is over us. Conversely, it has been demonstrated that the lower we hold someone in esteem, the less their influence is going to be. By "bringing someone down" through ridicule, criticism, finding fault, being judgmental and focusing on their shortcomings, the less control they have over you. This is evident in many situations. An executive who has distanced himself from his employees will have greater influence in this setting than the more intimate atmosphere of home where he lets his hair down and is perceived more realistically, faults and all. It is one of the reasons many political leaders avoid getting too close to their followers, teachers maintain a distance with students, and even lovers guard their space.

Your perceptions of the status of another then will make a difference in this person's degree of influence over you. Another significant variable is the spatial distance of the Authority Voice. The closer the proximity of the voice, the greater will be the control over your behavior. If the voice commands can be made to appear to "come from within", the depths of you, so much the better.

This prop is a little more difficult to set up than **Endless Tape Dynamics** but is definitely worth making the effort. Since you want to have control over The Voice (what it says, where, and when), the best procedure is to get it down on an audio-cassette tape for your convenience in playing. Your first task is to find someone whom you hold in high esteem (a friend, colleague, relative or public figure) and who has a strong, confident voice. Provide him or her with a short, blank cassette tape (no more than twenty minutes) and ask him/her to do the script on page 260 for you. Instruct your authority person to speak loudly, sincerely and with as much conviction as possible.

When you play it back later in your home or office, you want the voice messages to be as close in physical proximity to you as possible. Therefore, position your cassette player right next to where you are sitting or lying. Whenever possible use earphones and play it back in stereo. Turn the tone down on your cassette player and adjust the volume to a moderately loud, but not uncomfortable, level.

Note that through making use of this procedure, we have come full circle in taking charge of our lives—from being ruled by the ancient irrational voices within to looking outward for direction from external gods, kings and leaders, to finally bringing control back within by creating our own self-made script—this time according to the outcome we have elected.

As you gain prosperity confidence, another option is to experiment with using your own voice as The Authority. Compare its effectiveness with that of others. Make use of this technique as a supplement to the **Endless Tape Dynamics**. Both are dramatically effective desire-and-action generators.

Authoritarian Voice Script

(1)You believe in yourself and can do whatever you decide.

(2)You are capable of handling any situation.

(3)You see problems as opportunities.

(4)You can be counted on to do your best.

(5)You believe in your projects.

(6)You act in a manner to maximize the odds for a favorable outcome.

(7)There is a stride of confidence in the way you carry yourself.

(8)You take whatever steps are necessary to insure success.

(9)You speak and walk with confidence.

(10)You follow through on projects.

(11)When something needs to be done, you move quickly and effectively.

(12)Whatever it takes, you get the job done.

(13)You persevere IN SPITE OF anything that gets in the way.

(14)You recognize the value of your PPP.

(15)Every tiny detail of your PPP is important.

(16)You have a creative mission to fulfill in life that no one else can do.

Note: You can elaborate on these concepts and make them more specific to your goals. In making changes, be sure to keep them positive and stated in the present tense.

Guideline 5.
Prepare In Advance For Down Days

Recognize that there will be times when you are not moving ahead at full speed. Inertia, procrastination and stifling moods can creep up on you almost without warning. They might be related to a change in diet, lack of exercise, bad news or a sudden turn of events. The difference between success and failure is learning how to promptly reverse these moods before they get a grip on you and waste your time. It is much easier to pull yourself up and get going if you have done some advance preparation. You cannot expect to have the enthusiasm and energy to do an about face when you are at low ebb unless you have done some previous planning.

As an entrepreneur in charge of your own time, you no longer have an employer or boss standing over you, telling you what to do or setting up work incentives and reinforcements to keep you going. While your most potent long term motivator is the commitment, challenge and self-sustaining rewards of your PPP, intermittent, short-term "shots in the arm" help you stay on course. It is up to you to discover which props give you the biggest jolt and shake you out of any temporary ennui or depression that threatens your success. Here are five suggestions to turn your mood around on those days when you are feeling down and out.

(1)Arrange to receive surprise gifts

Give a friend, relative or business colleague some dollars and ask them to buy you a few surprise gifts. They could be amusing, novelty items or a special purchase you have been wanting. For example, a bright mod scarf, a pair of earrings, a sharp money clip, or one of the new children's computer toys that adults have so much fun with: crazy, talking animals, space robots, and dancing puppets. It needn't be anything expensive. Have your friend wrap them up for you and when you are feeling out of sorts and need a lift, open one up.

I have found this booster to be more effective for women than men (I'm not sure why), however, the right choice of gift along with the element of surprise can put a spark back in almost anyone's day.

(2)Listen to some upbeat, inspiring music

Don't leave this to chance by flipping on the radio and expecting to hear the kind of tunes you need. It has always been a mystery to me why someone who is feeling depressed will turn on the radio and listen to a steady diet of nostalgic, wailing love songs. "He doesn't love me anymore...lonely...I'm so sad and lonely...". This sort of mood masochism only serves to feed and reinforce any feelings of despair, defeat or disillusionment you already have.

Instead, have albums or cassettes handy that give you a lift and the energy you need. Music and rhythm are mighty stimulants which can turn most people's moods around in an instant, in either direction, up or down! A little reflection will tell you which of those tunes you already are familiar with give you a lift or a letdown.

(3)Sing

Besides listening to music, prod yourself to sing. It doesn't matter whether you can carry a tune or not. Humming and singing some bouncy, cheery lyrics is totally incompatible with feeling depressed, upset and staying on your duff doing nothing. Assuredly, you may not feel like singing, nonetheless taking the initiative here will pay off and get you back on the prosperity path in no time.

(4)Fast-talk yourself

Use self-talk and deal immediately with any problems that threaten to dampen your spirit. To reduce the destructive impact on yourself it is imperative that you learn to react instantly at a conscious level. When something goes wrong, rather than burying it, train yourself to say: "Okay, that was a rotten thing to happen but it's all right. I can take care of it." Next, consider what action (if any) is called for to improve the situation. After you have figured out whatever needs to be done, mentally let go of it.

Most of the things that happen to us are not real calamities. It's the minor day-to-day irritations and frustrations that are usually the demons in getting us down. Handle these quickly by reaching a decision about how you are going to react. This will knock out the negative emotional impact and keep it from surfacing later. Otherwise, the cumulative effect of a mess of unresolved incidents will leave you forever walking around with an unpleasant aftertaste.

(5)Have a tape on hand that gives you a personal pep talk

While there are many motivational cassette tapes on the market which are available to rent or purchase, you know yourself best and can make one adapted especially for your needs. Here is a sample script to get you started:

"All right, JJ, you may not think so right now, but this is going to be a FANTASTIC DAY. You are going to get up and go about your business bursting with enthusiasm and energy...in fact, your energy is absolutely going to abound! You know this can happen and it IS happening THIS INSTANT.

"Think back to a time in your life when you felt really wretched. The dragons of gloom were having a field day in your head, then BAM, all of a sudden you received some good news and just like that, you felt like you were floating on Cloud 9.

"Well, here's the good news. You have that high-flying happy mood built into you and have the power to call it up at will, WHENEVER YOU CHOOSE! Think about that. You NEVER have to be depressed again. It's entirely up to you. Within your personality is a whole bag of emotions: joy, elation, love, as well as boredom, apathy, resentment, anger. You can pull out whichever one you want, JUST BY MAKING THAT DECISION.

"How do you think actors perform? They call up whatever emotion that's right, whatever is appropriate, and put on a face of sadness, remorse, anger or joy, happiness and enthusiasm.

"In fact, we're all actors and actresses, and we tend to put on the face, the emotion, that we feel is appropriate in reacting to the circumstances in our lives. If something unpleasant or something you do not like happens (and you can be certain it will), remember you always have a choice about how you are going to interpret these events and respond to them.

"When things go wrong, you have every right to get upset, sit around and mope, and let it ruin the rest of your day or week or life. Certainly anyone would agree that you're justified in letting loose a torrent of negative emotions under many circumstances. But why bother? Whose needs are you serving, anyway? What good is sitting around in a state of gloom all day? There are always going to be things happening out there which you do not especially like...with different degrees of awfulness.

"Decide NOW to act in your own best interest, get your bones in gear and get going."

Putting together a tape for yourself tailored to your particular needs and idiosyncrasies is half the battle. It's fun to do and once you have the time invested you are more likely to be persuaded by the messages.

As you see, cassette tapes can be used for your prosperity in a variety of ways. Form the practice of making them a regular part of each day for inspiration, motivation and instruction.

The main idea with all of the suggestions under Guideline 5 is to have these remedies preplanned and readily, easily available when you need them. You know yourself best and with a little brainstorming and using the above recommendations as a springboard you should be able to come up with even more strategies to speedily jostle yourself out of a bad day so you can get on with your projects. By getting in the habit of making a game of our sour moods and downdrifts, we can keep the spirit of playfulness alive and well in our lives.

Time Block No. 21 summarizes the action-steps you need to take to turn down days around.

Time Block No. 21
Triumph Over Down Days

(1)Arrange to receive surprise gifts.
Block out a convenient time in your calendar the end of this week to contact a close friend or relative and give them $10.00 to $100.00 to purchase you some surprise gifts. Perhaps they would like you to do the same for them in exchange!

(2)Listen to some upbeat, inspiring music.
This evening check the recordings you have available at home. If none of these are suitable, block out a time in your calendar this week to go to the record shop and purchase one.

(3)Sing.
Make a list of a few cheery songs that you know the lyrics to. Do this now. If you don't know any, schedule time to pick up some music sheets at the same time you go to the record shop.

(4)Fast-talk yourself.
Write down ONE KEY COMMAND to say to yourself when something goes wrong. It should be brief, positive, forceful and convincing. State it out loud to yourself now.

(5)Have a tape on hand that gives you a personal pep talk.
Block out one hour this weekend to create a personalized tape. Use the dialogue provided in the example given to get started. It's easy and fun!

###############

Staying Fused With A Playful, Creative Spirit
On-Going Time Blocks

Time Block No. 19
Endless Tape Dynamics

Play this tape for fifteen minutes each morning when you first awaken and fifteen minutes each night before you drift off to sleep. Block out the time for a minimum of five days per week for the next six weeks.

Time Block No. 20
Voices of Authority

Play this tape for five minutes each day, seven days per week. It is best played at midday when you have a few minutes free. Otherwise play it at night prior to the Endless Tape script.

Block these times out in your calendar now!

V
Epilogue

Epilogue

"Nothing splendid has ever been achieved except by those who dared believe that something inside them was superior to circumstances."

—BRUCE BARTON

Both riches and happiness abound in the process of discovering and fulfilling your creative mission through entrepreneurship. You allow this to happen by learning to view each elusive time element (hours, minutes, seconds) as your own personal great gift from the universe, available for molding in as many remarkable ways as you wish.

As you leave the occupational baggage behind, you go forth taking the helm to shape your circumstances and construct a personal and business world from your inner stirrings of truth, vision, playfulness and passion; a world that comes alive by virtue of your touch and special blend of human yearnings and interests. Herein lies the future and hope for each individual and nation.

ORDER FORM

QTY.	BOOK	PRICE EACH
	PLAY AND GROW RICH Jan Gault *(2nd Ed., 271 pgs., illus., soft cover 10-7/8 X 8-3/8, ISBN 0-923699-00-7)*	**$22.95***
	If California resident, add 7-1/4% sales tax ($1.66)	
	Add $3.50 shipping & handling for single book orders or $2 each for multiple book orders; Canada send additional $1.75	
	TOTAL	

Δ I have enclosed my check or money order

Please make checks payable to:

Uptime Enterprises
P.O. Box 612700
So. Lake Tahoe, California 96152

(PLEASE PRINT)

Name____

Address______________________________City____________________

State__________ZIP________Phone(s)__________________________

Charge to: ΔVISA Account No.______________________________

ΔMasterCard Expires__________

Signature________________________________

***"Play & Grow Rich" makes a great gift. Why not order an extra copy for a friend, relative or colleague?**

*Discounts are available on large quantities for your group or organization. Please write or telephone for pricing information.

FOR INFORMATION ABOUT SEMINARS, AUDIO/VIDEO CASSETTE TAPES & BOOKS, WRITE:

Notes